# The Lighthouse Companion
## for
## Maine

*Photographs by Paul Rezendes*

Published by Tide-mark Press
Windsor, Connecticut

Published by Tide-mark Press Ltd.
P.O. Box 20, Windsor, CT 06095

Printed in Korea by Samhwa Printing Co.

Design and typography by Paul Rasid

Library of Congress Control Number: 2005924139

ISBN 1-59490-004-3

First Edition/First Printing

# Contents

# Maine Lighthouses

*West Quoddy Head Light, Lubec, Maine*

Maine has more than sixty existing lighthouses—including the nation's easternmost lighthouse—marking the many harbors, islands, rocky ledges, and riverbanks of its over 3,000 miles of shoreline. Maine's lighthouses and their keepers have endured cold ocean winds, snowstorms, heavy fog, and the highest tides in the continental United States. Most of these light stations are active aids to navigation—a testament to their longevity and functionality in this age of depth finders and global positioning systems. With their distinctive markings and lighting patterns, Maine's light stations warn both commercial vessels and pleasure boats of dangers and establish locations, helping sailors find their way through fog, storms, and dark of night.

Dating back as far as the Revolutionary War, Maine lighthouses were sometimes a part of history as it unfolded, bearing silent witness to horrible tragedies as well as heartwarming stories of lives saved. Some lighthouses still display 200-year-old armament on the property, reminding us of a day when we defended our shores. Others suffered damage at the hands of the enemy. Light keepers have often been known to go above and beyond the duty of keeping the light lit, risking their own lives to pull others out of the freezing water, sometimes with the aid of wives, children, and at least once, a dog. Let this guide take you on a tour of Maine's lighthouses, and discover their romance and history for yourself.

# Maine Lighthouse Locations by Number

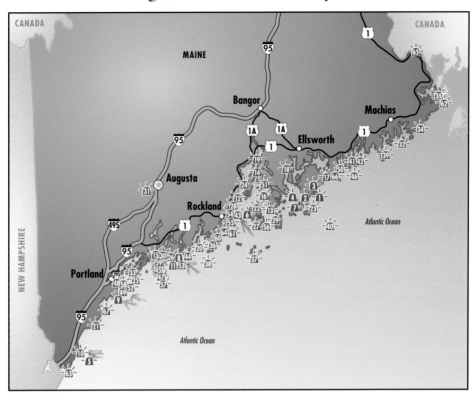

# Baker Island Light

Baker Island, a small, rocky island at the southwestern entrance to Frenchman Bay, was pioneered by William and Hannah Gilley in the early 19th century. When John Quincy Adams ordered a lighthouse to be built on the island in 1828 to warn mariners of the shoals around the five Cranberry Isles and the sandbar adjacent to Little Cranberry Island, William Gilley was appointed keeper at a salary of $350 per year.

# Baker Island Light

## The Cranberry Isles, Maine

The Gilley family prospered on the island, despite the challenges of isolation and self-sufficiency. William Gilley served as light keeper for 20 years before being ousted in 1849 for not belonging to the dominant Whig party. Though offered an opportunity to retain his position if he were to switch political allegiances, it is said that Gilley stated he would not switch political parties "for all the lighthouses in the United States." Thus, he moved to nearby Great Duck Island, though many of his children remained and eventually raised their own families on Baker Island.

Today, Baker Island Light remains an active aid to navigation, though it is maintained by the National Park Service as part of Acadia National Park. In addition to the tower, which was replaced in 1855 with a 43-foot cylindrical brick tower equipped with a fourth-order Fresnel lens, visitors can see the keeper's quarters, oil house, fuel house, and two storage buildings.

## Directions

Baker Island Light is located at the southwest entrance of Frenchman Bay on the opposite side of the Cranberry Isles. It is viewable only by boat. There are no park-organized tours of the light, but private charters are available. The station is only open to the public in the summer.

Latitude: 44° 14' 30" N
Longitude: 68° 11' 54" W

Contact Information:
Acadia National Park
Box 177
Bar Harbor, ME 04609
(207) 288-3338
www.nps.gov/acad

# Bass Harbor Head Light

Built in 1858 on a rocky hill on Mount Desert Island, Bass Harbor Head Light marks the entrance to Blue Hill Bay and Bass Harbor, particularly the sand bar at Bass Harbor. It is southwest of the Cranberry Isles on Acadia National Park property. One of Maine's most photographed lighthouses, Bass Harbor Head Light attracts legions of visitors from both near and far.

The light station at Bass Harbor Head is the original structure, built of stone and brick in a cylindrical tower with the original wood-frame keeper's quarters still attached. Originally equipped with a fifth-order Fresnel lens, the current working lens is a fourth-order Fresnel installed in 1902. It has a red light occulting every 4 seconds. The tower is 32 feet tall with a focal plane at 56 feet above sea level. The station is equipped with a fog bell, but it is inactive. Owned by the U.S. Coast Guard, Bass Harbor Head Light is still an active aid to navigation.

Because they house Coast Guard staff, the keeper's quarters are not open to the public, although the grounds are.

# Bass Harbor Head Light

**Bass Harbor, Maine**

## Directions

Take I-95 to Bangor. Take Route 1A south to Ellsworth. Take Route 3 east/south to Mount Desert Island. Take Route 102 south to Southwest Harbor, about 10 miles from the head of the island. Go through Southwest Harbor and take Route 102A south. Go about 6 miles to the turn to the lighthouse; it is about a mile down.

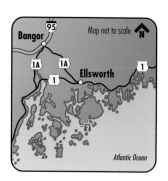

Latitude: 44° 13' 18" N
Longitude: 68° 20' 12" W

**Contact Information:**
**U.S. Coast Guard Aides**
**to Navigation Team**
**P.O. Box 5000**
**Southwest Harbor, ME 04679**
**www.uscg.mil**

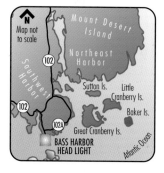

# Bear Island Light

Bear Island Light was designed at its inception in 1839 as a family lighthouse, and at one point even hosted a family pet—a dog named Cleo owned by Terry Stanley, who served as keeper of the beacon in the 1950s.

Ordered by President Van Buren in 1839, the first structure, made of stone with a tower on top, burned in 1852. It was replaced by 1853, but in 1889, because the building was badly decayed, the current brick structure was built on the order of President Harrison.

Though family lights were a coveted property for Coast Guard keepers, Bear Island Light was deactivated in 1981 and became the property of Acadia National Park. In 1989, the park established a long-term lease of the property to a private owner, who, along with the Friends of Acadia, has refurbished the property to make it suitable for occupancy. The 3.4-acre property consists of a two-story, 31-foot light tower complete with a fifth-order Fresnel lens. Also on the premises are the keeper's quarters, a stone oil house, a barn, and a boathouse.

# Bear Island Light

## The Cranberry Isles, Maine

### Directions

The lighthouse is privately leased and not open to the public. Though there is no place to land a craft, the lighthouse can be seen from the water. Charters are available out of Northeast Harbor.

Latitude: 44° 17' 00" N
Longitude: 68° 16' 12" W

**Contact Information:**
Acadia National Park
Box 177
Bar Harbor, ME 04609
(207) 288-3338
www.nps.gov/acad

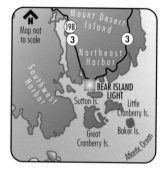

# Blue Hill Bay Light

Built on a very small, rocky tract of land known as Green Island, Blue Hill Bay Light was erected in 1857 by order of President Pierce. Also known as Eggemoggin Light, Blue Hill Bay Light marks the entrance to Blue Hill Bay as well as Eggemoggin Reach, which connects Blue Hill Bay with Penobscot Bay. In the 19th century the area was a busy place for shippers of ice and lumber and was popular with tourists, as well.

The 22-foot, cylindrical brick tower was originally equipped with a fourth-order Fresnel lens that shone 26 feet above sea level. The light was deactivated in 1933 and replaced in 1935 by a skeleton tower with a solar-powered optic that flashes green every 4 seconds. Now used as a private home, the original light is attached to the wood-frame, Cape Cod–style keeper's quarters by a small brick chartroom. There is just enough room on the island for the boathouse and oil house built in 1905.

# Blue Hill Bay Light

### Also known as Eggemoggin Light
### Green Island, Maine

## Directions

Blue Hill Bay Light is located on Green Island in Blue Hill Bay, 3.7 miles southeast of Brooklin. It is not viewable from land. The property is privately owned and not open to the public.

Latitude: 44° 14' 54" N
Longitude: 68° 29' 54" W

**Contact Information:**
**Privately owned.**

# Boon Island Light

In 1710, the British merchant ship *Nottingham Galley* ran aground, stranding Captain John Deanne and his sailors and forcing them to resort to cannibalism for survival. This is just one tragic tale in the history of the ironically named Boon Island—and one of the reasons Boon Island Light was established in 1779.

Not much more than a flat, 700-foot-long rock outcropping about 9 miles off the coast of York, Boon Island and its lighthouse were vulnerable to Mother Nature's tempests. The original tower, built in 1799, was washed from the flat, isolated island in 1804 and not replaced until 1811, when a 25-foot structure was built. In 1831 that structure was washed away, as well, and its replacement was so small, it was hardly noticeable. In 1855, the 133-foot, cylindrical granite tower we see now was built.

In later years, storms continued to do powerful damage, both to the lighthouse and its inhabitants. One mid-19th-century keeper brought his young bride to accompany him on his assignment. One stormy night the keeper fell ill, and the young woman kept vigil by his side, taking breaks only to keep the tower lighted, knowing lives depended on it. Sadly, her husband died, and despondent over her loss, she lost her strength and was found a few days later, wandering and demented.

Two lightkeepers were present at the lighthouse during the Blizzard of 1978. During the storm the keeper's quarters, supply building, and boat house were all blown off the island, leaving the men nowhere to take shelter but the lantern room. After the men were rescued the next day, the light was automated so no more lives would be endangered.

Originally equipped with a second-order Fresnel lens, Boon Island Light now has a VEGA VRB-25 solar-powered automated optic that shines 137 feet above sea level, flashes white every 5 seconds, and can be seen for 19 miles.

### Directions

Boon Island Light is best seen by boat. Charters are available out of Portsmouth or Rye, New Hampshire. In addition, a distant view is possible from the Cape Neddick (Nubble) Light. From I-95 outside of York, take exit 4 and travel east to Route 1. Go north to Nubble Road and turn east. Take Nubble Road to Sohier Park to view both Boon Island Light and Cape Neddick (Nubble) Light. The tower is not open to the public.

Latitude: 43° 07' 18" N
Longitude: 70° 28' 36" W

**Contact Information:**
**American Lighthouse Foundation**
**P.O. Box 889**
**Wells, ME 04090**
**(207) 646-0245**
**www.lighthousefoundation.org**

# Browns Head Light

Serving Vinalhaven Island's fishing, lobstering, and granite industries since before the Civil War, Browns Head Light has always been a popular sight-seeing attraction. In the early days, keepers were 6 or 7 miles from the nearest town and they welcomed visits from tourists and vacationers.

Browns Head Light is located on the northwest side of the island in Penob-scot Bay. Established in 1832 by order of President Jackson, the original rubblestone tower was replaced with the current 20-foot, black-and-white brick cylindrical tower in 1857 by order of President Buchanan. The original fifth-order Fresnel lens was replaced by a fourth-order lens in 1902. That lens, still in use today, shines a continuous white light at 39 feet above sea level, making it visible for up to 14 miles.

When the light became automated in 1987, the town of Vinalhaven began leasing the property from the Coast Guard so it wouldn't be vandalized or otherwise fall into disrepair. Though the wood tower that housed the fog bell has been dismantled, the original 1857 keeper's quarters are in modern condition. Also on the site is an oil house that was built in 1903. Today, the lighthouse serves as home to Vinalhaven's town manager, who splits duties between working at the town hall and running the lighthouse. The lighthouse grounds are open to the public; however, the town asks that visitors respect the privacy of the lighthouse's inhabitants.

### Directions

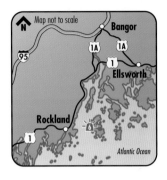

To get to the Maine State Ferry Service from Route 1 in Rockland, go to Main Street and turn right. Turn right on North Haven Road. Turn left on Crockett River Road and then turn right on Browns Head Light Road. For more information on the ferry, visit www.state.me.us/mdot/opt/ferry.

Coming off the ferry, turn left onto Sands Road and follow it to the end. Turn right on Dog Town Road and follow a slight left onto North Haven Road. There is a side road on the right, across from an electrical station; follow that and the signs to the lighthouse.

Latitude: 44° 06' 42" N
Longitude: 68° 54' 36" W

**Contact:**
**Town of Vinalhaven**
**North Main Street**
**Vinalhaven, ME 04863**
**(207) 863-4471**

# Burnt Coat Harbor Light

Built on Hockamock Head, a high point on Swans Island, Burnt Coat Harbor Light was constructed in 1872 by order of President Grant. Serving fishing boats and cargo vessels for years in the Swans Island area, the light was once part of a pair of range lights. Because of complaints from mariners that the differing sizes and arrangement of the two towers were confusing, the Lighthouse Department had the smaller tower taken down in 1885.

With a tower height of 32 feet, Burnt Coat Harbor Light shines at 75 feet above sea level for a range of 9 miles. It continues to serve as an active aid to navigation. It was originally equipped with a fourth-order Fresnel, but now has a 250-mm lens that shines a white light occulting every 4 seconds. In addition to the tower, the 1911 fog signal building still exists, but is inactive. The original 1872 keeper's quarters and an oil house also still stand on the property. Plans are in the works to restore these buildings and turn the area into a public park.

# Burnt Coat Harbor Light

### Also Known as Hockamock Head Light
### Swans Island, Maine

## Directions

Take the ferry to Swans Island. From the ferry property, go south (right) off Ferry Road on to Atlantic Road. Follow it to Harbor Road and go south to Lighthouse Road. Take Lighthouse Road to the harbor, which is on the left.

Latitude: 44° 08' 06" N
Longitude: 68° 26' 42" W

**Contact Information:**
Town of Swans Island
Harbor Road
Swans Island, ME 04685
(207) 526-4279

# Burnt Island Light

One of the oldest existing lighthouses in America, this conical stone structure marking the entrance to busy Boothbay Harbor was built in 1821. In addition to providing a much-needed service to mariners entering and exiting the harbor, the lighthouse won acclaim throughout the state for its beauty. The *Boothbay Register* even proclaimed the beacon to be "one of the most beautiful harbor lighthouses on the entire Atlantic Coast."

Because of the condition of the property and its proximity to town, this was a desirable assignment for keepers, particularly those with families. However, the low maintenance of the facility demanded only one keeper, so positions were limited.

The whitewashed, 31-foot rubblestone tower originally housed Lewis Patent reflectors, but a 300-mm lens is now in operation and shines a flashing red beam 61 feet above sea level for a range of 15 miles every 6 seconds. The 1895 fog bell building has been dismantled, but the 1857 keeper's quarters still stand, as do an oil house, covered walkway, boathouse, fuel house, barn, and hen house.

# Burnt Island Light

## Southport, Maine

On June 20, 1998, the Maine Department of Marine Resources purchased Burnt Island Light as part of the Maine Lights program. Five years later to the day, the Burnt Island Living Lighthouse was dedicated. This program features an educational curriculum that focuses on topics relating to Maine's maritime heritage, coastal environment, marine fisheries, and conservation. The lighthouse and associated buildings have all been restored. While open to the public for tours, Burnt Island Light remains an active aid to navigation.

## Directions

From Wiscasset, take Highway 1 north across the Sheepscot River. Go south on Route 27 to Boothbay Harbor, about 12 miles. Continue on Route 27 south to Southport. Take Route 238 south to Capital Island Road. Turn left on Capital Island Road, from along which one can see the lighthouse. Alternatively, a charter can be booked out of Boothbay Harbor or Bath. The Maine Department of Marine Resources offers tours and cruises (see contact information below).

Latitude: 43° 49' 30" N
Longitude: 69° 38' 24" W

Contact Information:
Maine Department of Marine Resources
Education Division
P.O. Box 8
W. Boothbay Harbor, ME 04575
(207) 633-9559
www.state.me.us/dmr

# Cape Elizabeth Light

Built high on Cape Elizabeth, Cape Elizabeth Light station consists of what was once a pair of lighthouses built by congressional order in 1827 to replace a daytime monument erected in 1811.

The twin lighthouses remained until 1874, when they were deemed too worn for safe use and replaced by two cast-iron structures 300 yards apart. Though little visual evidence supports the claim, it is said that at one time, for daytime identification purposes, the west tower was painted with one large, vertical red stripe, and the east tower was painted with four horizontal red stripes. The west tower was deactivated in 1924.

The remaining east tower, shown here, is 67 feet tall and shines 129 feet above sea level for a range of 15 miles. Its original second-order Fresnel lens was replaced in 1994 with an FA-251 lens, which was in turn replaced by a VRB-25 aerobeacon. The light flashes white four times every 15 seconds.

Cape Elizabeth Light station is no stranger to drama. One particularly harrowing event took place in the winter of 1885 when a large schooner ran aground on the cape in a snowstorm. Already worn from attending his duties

# Cape Elizabeth Light

**Also known as Two Lights**
**Cape Elizabeth, Maine**

while ill, the keeper further risked his life to save two crewmembers from falling to their deaths and/or freezing to death.

### Directions

From I-95, take exit 7 and go straight off the ramp to Route 1 (Main Street). Turn north (left) on Route 1 and go to Broadway. Bear right on Broadway but stay left. Follow Broadway to Route 77. Turn south on Route 77 to Two Lights Road, a distance of 4–5 miles. Turn left on Two Lights Road and look for the lighthouse to the west. The lighthouse and grounds are not open to the public.

Latitude: 43° 34' 00" N
Longitude: 70° 12' 00" W

**Contact:**
**American Lighthouse Foundation**
**P.O. Box 889**
**Wells, ME 04090**
**(207) 646-0245**
**www.lighthousefoundation.org**

## Cape Neddick Light

Located on the north side of what fishermen have for many years called the "Nubble," a promontory located a mere 600 feet off the coast of York, Cape Neddick Light was ordered by President Hayes in 1879. The view from the light tower includes unusual rock formations known as Bald Head Cliff, the Devil's Oven, and Pulpit Rock.

The 41-foot, cast-iron tower seen today is the original, built in 1879. The original fourth-order Fresnel lens was replaced in 1928 with another fourth-order lens only a few years younger. Its red light flashes red 4 seconds on, 4 seconds off, and shines at 88 feet above sea level for a range of 13 miles. The station was automated in 1987.

The two-story Victorian keeper's quarters built in 1879 still stand, making the property very picturesque. The sound signal building has been dismantled, but the eye-catching red oil house, storage building, and boathouse are

# Cape Neddick Light

**Also known as Nubble Light**
**York, Maine**

still standing. Also of note at the site is a cable pulley system that runs from the mainland to the island. Used for many years to transport supplies from the mainland to Cape Neddick Light, it also carried a more unusual type of cargo in the 1960s, when keeper David Winchester would use the bucket to send his son to school on the mainland each day.

## Directions

From I-95 outside of York, take exit 4 and travel east to Route 1. Go south on Route 1 to Route 1A and turn east. Go to Nubble Road and turn right. Take Nubble Road to Sohier Park to view both Boon Island Light and Cape Neddick (Nubble) Light.

Latitude: 43° 09' 54" N
Longitude: 70° 35' 30" W

**Contact Information:**
**Friends of Nubble Light**
**186 York Street**
**York, ME 03909**
**www.yorkmaine.org**

# The Cuckolds Light

Originally a tripod daytime marker, the Cuckolds station was established in 1892. Because the area was becoming increasingly heavily trafficked, a fog station was added shortly thereafter; it consisted only of a compressed-air signal for 15 years. In 1907, under the approval of President Roosevelt, a tower was built on top of the fog signal building. Built on a granite base, the light has a 48-foot tower and shines at 59 feet above sea level for 12 miles.

Living quarters were tight at this family station and keepers were entitled to only two days of shore leave a month. Furthermore, trips to the main-land were dependent on both the availability of Coast Guard vessels and the weather. "It takes a sturdy relationship to endure that much togetherness," said one former lightkeeper. "I guess lighthouses are romantic but I do know that this one had quite a reputation concerning the couples that stayed there and the divorce rate."

Originally fitted with a fourth-order Fresnel lens, the light now has a VRB-25 that flashes white twice every 6 seconds. The original fog signal still operates and a radio beacon has been added. The keeper's quarters were destroyed by a blizzard in 1978.

# The Cuckolds Light

## Southport, Maine

### Directions

Cuckolds Light is not open to the public and is best viewed from the water. Charters are available out of Bath or Boothbay Harbor.

Latitude: 43° 46' 48" N
Longitude: 69° 39' 00" W

**Contact Information:**
**U.S. Coast Guard**
**Aides to Navigation Team**
**P.O. Box 5000**
**Southwest Harbor, ME**
**04679**
**www.uscg.mil**

# Curtis Island Light

Once called Negro Island after an African cook who lived there, Curtis Island was renamed for Cyrus H. K. Curtis, publisher of the *Saturday Evening News*, philanthropist, and longtime Camden resident. Curtis Island sits at the entrance to Camden Harbor, with an excellent view of Mount Batty and Mount Megunticook.

The station was established in 1836 under President Jackson, but the lighthouse was rebuilt in 1896 by order of President Cleveland. The 1896 light was equipped with a fourth-order Fresnel lens, but it now has a 300-mm solar-powered automated signal with a green light that occults every 4 seconds. The tower height is 25 feet and the light shines at 52 feet above sea level for a range of 8 miles.

Keeper's quarters dating from 1889 still stand, as do a barn, oil house, boathouse, and catwalk. When the light was automated in 1972, the town of Camden gained control of the lighthouse. In 1997, the town officially purchased the lighthouse through the Maine Lights program. It is an active aid to navigation and part of a town park that is accessible only to boaters.

# Curtis Island Light

### Camden, Maine

### Directions

From Highway 1 in Camden, travel south on Bay View Street to Camden Harbor. The lighthouse is located to the south. For a closer look, it may be useful to book a boat tour out of Camden or view the light from a private boat.

Latitude: 44° 12' 06" N
Longitude: 69° 02' 54" W

**Contact Information:**
Town of Camden
P.O. Box 1207
Camden, ME 04843
(207) 236-3353

# Deer Island Thorofare Light

Built in 1857 to meet demand from sailors in the Deer Island area, Deer Island Thorofare Light is located on the west side of Mark Island and marks (naturally) the Deer Island Thorofare. During the mid-19th century, this area was heavily trafficked by fishermen and deepwater traders serving the granite industry.

The 25-foot, square tower is the original granite structure that was ordered to replace or supplement the buoys that had previously warned mariners of the many islands around Penobscot Bay. Originally equipped with a fourth-order Fresnel lens, the light was automated in 1958 and now has a 250-mm solar-powered lens. The light shines at 52 feet above sea level and flashes white every 6 seconds.

A 1908 sound signal building was dismantled in the 1970s. The original keeper's quarters burned in 1959 and were not replaced. There are, how-ever, a boathouse, oil house, and storage building on the site. In 1997, Deer Island Thorofare Light was purchased by Island Heritage Trust through the Maine Lights program. In addition to working to preserve the lighthouse, which continues to serve as an active aid to navigation, the Trust plans to turn Mark Island into a wildlife refuge.

# Deer Island Thorofare Light

**Also known as Mark Island Light**
**Stonington, Maine**

## Directions

From Orland, take Route 15 south to Route 199. Go right toward Penobscot. Turn left on Route 175 and go through Penobscot. Get back on Route 15 south and go past the bridge in Deer Isle. In Deer Island, go south on Sunset Road and follow it to Sand Beach Road. Turn right on Sand Beach Road and there will be multiple opportunities for viewing the lighthouse. The station is not open to the public.

Latitude: 44° 08' 06" N
Longitude: 68° 42' 12" W

**Contact Information:**
**Island Heritage Trust**
**P.O. Box 42**
**Deer Isle, ME 04627**
**(207) 348-2455**
**www.mltn.org**

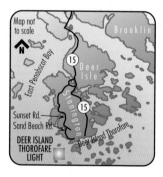

# Dice Head Light

Located well into Penobscot Bay on the tip of a peninsula outside the mouth of the Penobscot River, Dice Head Light was built in 1828 by order of President Jackson. Because of the importance of the area to the shipping and fishing industries, President Buchanan ordered it remodeled in 1858. The original tower was equipped with a Lewis Patent lens that shone at 130 feet above sea level. It was constructed of stone, which was common for early-19th-century lighthouses.

# Dice Head Light

**Also known as Dyce Head Light**
**Castine, Maine**

According to some sources, it was the beam of Dice Head Light that guided Maine pilot Bill Wincapaw to safety during a December 1929 storm. In appreciation for the services of the Dice Head keeper and dedicated keepers throughout all of Maine, Wincapaw made a special flight that Christmas, dropping gifts in front of each lighthouse for the keepers and their families. This began a tradition known as the "Flying Santa" that continues even today.

Although deactivated in 1937, the original lighthouse still stands near the skeletal, 27-foot automated tower that was built to replace it. The keeper's residence, now owned by the town of Castine, is leased out to private owners to help cover the costs of maintenance. Though damaged in a 1999 fire, work is underway to restore the quarters to their original state.

## Directions

From Highway 1 near Orland, turn south on Highway 175 and drive for 8 miles to West Penobscot. From there, continue south on Highway 166 for roughly 7 miles to Castine. In Castine, follow Battle Avenue past the Maine Maritime Academy to the street's end. The keeper's house is a private residence, but there is a public path leading to the light.

Latitude: 44° 22' 54" N
Longitude: 68° 49' 12" W

**Contact Information:**
**Town of Castine**
P.O. Box 204
Castine, ME 04421
(207) 326-4502
www.castine.me.us

# Doubling Point Light

Like the several light stations along the Kennebec River, Doubling Point Light was built to help shippers and fishermen from Bath, known as the "City of Ships" because of its long maritime history, make their way up the busy waterway.

Located near the upper part of Fiddlers Reach, the lighthouse sits out on a dock that provides a walkway through the marsh. The 1899 octagonal, wooden lighthouse shines at 23 feet above sea level. Originally equipped with a lantern lens, a fifth-order Fresnel lens was installed in 1902. Doubling Point Light now has a 300-mm optic that flashes white every 4 seconds. In the 1980s, the responsibility of tending Doubling Point Light was designated to the keeper of the Doubling Point Range Lights. For a few years, Karen McLean, one of the few women lightkeepers in the nation, carried out this double duty.

The keeper's quarters built in 1898 still exist, as do the fogbell tower, oil house, and a storage building. Still an active aid to navigation, the property is now owned by the Friends of the Doubling Point Light. Since 1997, this nonprofit foundation has worked to restore and preserve the lighthouse

# Doubling Point Light

## Arrowsic, Maine

and its property. This has not been an easy feat. In 1998, the group had the entire structure lifted and relocated so that the crumbling granite base of the lighthouse could be repaired. The lighthouse was returned to its original site on January 5, 2000, though repairs continue.

### ⚓ Directions

Follow Route 1 west to the Bath Bridge; bear right (south) immediately east of the bridge. Turn left at the bottom of the hill and continue over the Arrowsic Bridge. Continue south on Route 127 for about 1 mile and turn right onto the road marked, "Whitmore's Landing, to Doubling Point Rd." At the "T" in the road, turn left onto Doubling Point Road, go past the stone wall, and follow this road to its end. The tower and keeper's quarters are not open to the public, although the grounds are.

Latitude: 43° 53' 00" N
Longitude: 69° 48' 24" W

**Contact Information:**
**Friends of Doubling Point Light**
**c/o Betsy Skillings-Coleman**
**HCR 33 Box 61B,**
**Arrowsic, ME 04530**
**www.doublingpoint.org**

# Eagle Island Light

Perched high above Penobscot Bay on Eagle Island, Eagle Island Light was built in 1838 to mark the Hardhead Shoals running from the mainland to Deer Isle.

A family station, Eagle Island Light came with its share of obstacles. Winters were cold and icy at Deer Isle, and keepers often could not travel to the mainland due to the harsh weather. Families stationed at the island before 1919 were not provided a boat for transportation, leaving them at the mercy of kindly passersby. Indoor plumbing and a well did not even exist at the station until the mid-1940s.

In 1959, Eagle Island Light was automated. Five years later, the Coast Guard razed the oil house, storage building, and outhouse. The crew lost control of the beacon's giant bell when removing it from the tower, and the giant instrument rolled into the sea; it was later rescued and put on display at Great Spruce Head Island.

The 1939, pyramid-shaped fogbell tower still stands on the property with the original 30-foot stone tower. The 1858 fourth-order Fresnel lens has

# Eagle Island Light

## Deer Isle, Maine

been replaced by a 300-mm solar-powered optic that shines at 106 feet above sea level and flashes white every 4 seconds. It can be seen from 9 miles away and is an active aid to navigation.

## Directions

Best seen by boat, the lighthouse is on the northeast tip of Eagle Island in East Penobscot Bay. Boats can be hired out of Deer Isle for those without personal crafts. The station is not open to the public.

Latitude: 44° 13' 06" N
Longitude: 68° 46' 06" W

**Contact Information:**
Eagle Light Caretakers
c/o Sam Howe
2742 Normandy Drive NW
Atlanta, GA 30305

# Egg Rock Light

Situated on a mass of ledges east of Mount Desert Island, Egg Rock Light marks the entrance to Frenchman Bay. Built in 1875 by order of President Grant, its 40-foot tower is constructed of brick, although the integrated keeper's quarters are made of wood.

Though battered by terrible storms in the 19th century, the brick building that housed the steam-powered fog signal still stands, as do an oil house, boathouse, and generator house. The original keeper's quarters, which were re-roofed in 1899, are part of the lighthouse tower.

Automated in 1976, Egg Rock's original fifth-order Fresnel lens was replaced by rotating aerobeacons and the lantern room was removed. This left the lighthouse looking incomplete, and public outcry led the Coast Guard to furbish the site with a new lantern and house in 1986. Today, a VRB-25 aerobeacon serves mariners by flashing red every 5 seconds and shining at 64 feet above sea level for a range of 18 miles.

Egg Rock Light is owned by the U.S. Fish and Wildlife Department and is managed by Petit Manan Wildlife Refuge. A protected nesting area for seabirds, the island is closed to the public during nesting season (April through August).

# Egg Rock Light

## Winter Harbor, Maine

### Directions

Take I-95 to Bangor, then take Route 1A south to Ellsworth. Take Route 3 east/south to Mount Desert Island. At the head of the island, stay on Route 3. Travel about 10 miles to the docks in Bar Harbor. The lighthouse can be seen from boats out of Bar Harbor, but it is not open to the public.

Latitude: 44° 21' 12" N
Longitude: 68° 08' 18" W

**Contact Information:**
**U.S. Fish and Wildlife Service**
**Petit Manan National Wildlife Refuge**
**P.O. Box 279**
**Milbridge, ME 04658**
**(207) 546-2124**
**http://petitmanan.fws.gov/**

# First Light Bed & Breakfast

The First Light Bed & Breakfast is located on the waterfront in East Blue Hill, overlooking scenic McHeard Cove. Built 30 years ago as a private residence, the property now serves as a privately run inn. There are three rooms at First Light, including the Lighthouse Suite, which is located up a flight of wooden stairs in a tower that resembles an authentic lighthouse. Once up the stairs, patrons are rewarded with a stunning 360-degree view through 5-foot windows. From here, visitors can view everything from the calm waters of McHeard Cove to the hills of Mount Desert Island.

Though never an active lighthouse, this is a site not to be missed!

# First Light Bed & Breakfast

## East Blue Hill, Maine

### Directions

From Bucksport, take Route 1 through Orland to Route 15 south. Take Route 15 south to Blue Hill and go left (east) on Route 176. Take the next right to stay on Route 176, also known as East Blue Hill Road. First Light Bed & Breakfast is 4 miles ahead on the right.

Latitude: N/A
Longitude: N/A

**Contact Information:**
First Light Bed & Breakfast
821 East Blue Hill Road
East Blue Hill, ME 04614
(207) 374-5879
www.firstlightbandb.com

# Fort Point Light

Built by order of President Jackson in 1836 at the entrance of the Penobscot River, Fort Point Light is named for Fort Pownal, which once occupied the land. In 1759, then Governor Pownal thought a fort on that spot was necessary for the same reason a lighthouse was necessary: Access to a major shipping line must be protected, either from the Native Americans and the French or from nature's elements. It was one of the first lights to be built along a river, away from the coast. The light marks the river for inhabitants of Stockton Springs, once a very busy lumbering community.

Though automated in 1988, the original 1837, fourth-order Fresnel lens is still in operation. The 1890 fogbell building remains intact, and the 1857 Cape Cod–style keeper's quarters still stand. There is also a barn dating back to 1890, a brick oil house, a garage, and a breezeway. The square brick tower, with a unique round interior staircase, stands at 31 feet and shines a fixed white light at 88 feet above sea level. It can be seen from 15 miles away and is an active aid to navigation.

Now part of Fort Point State Park, the property is being developed as a museum with the original bell tower on display. Terry Cole, a former keeper for Fort Point Light in the 1970s, now lives in the keeper's quarters with his family as a ranger at the park. Cole offers a tour and slide presentation of the lighthouse to school and tour groups with advance notice.

## Directions

From Highway 1 (West Main Street) in Stockton Springs, take Church Street south to East Main Street. Go left to Cape Jellison Road and turn right. Once on Cape Jellison, turn left on East Cape Road, continue for 1.6 miles, and make another left onto Fort Point Road, which leads to the lighthouse.

Latitude: 44° 28' 00" N
Longitude: 68° 48' 42" W

**Contact Information:**
**Fort Point State Historic Site**
**c/o Bureau of Parks and Lands**
**106 Hogan Road**
**Bangor, ME 04401**
**(207) 567-3356**
**www.state.me.us**

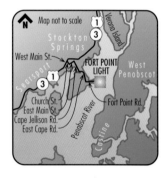

# Franklin Island Light

The third-oldest light station site in Maine, Franklin Island Light was built in 1803 by order of President Jefferson. Originally consisting of a day marker located on the northwest side of Franklin Island, it was hoped that this station would preclude wrecks on the small islets and shoals in the area. However, the marker was eventually found to be inadequate for the amount of coastal marine traffic during the mid-19th century.

In 1855, President Pierce ordered the day marker replaced by a 45-foot tower with a fourth-order Fresnel lens. That lens has since been replaced with a 250-mm, solar-powered lens that shines at 57 feet above sea level and flashes white every 6 seconds. Automated in 1967, the newer optic can be seen from 8 miles away. The original fourth-order Fresnel is now on display at the Boothbay Harbor Coast Guard Station. Franklin Island Light remains an active aid to navigation.

The keeper's quarters were dismantled in 1967 and there is no fog signal building; however, there is an oil house dating back to 1895. Since August 1999, a group called Franklin Light Preservation has maintained the property through a contract with the Coast Guard.

# Franklin Island Light

## Friendship, Maine

### Directions

Franklin Island Light is best seen by boat. There are private charters available out of Friendship, Rockland, and Boothbay Harbor. Please keep in mind that because the light is located on a wild-life refuge, it is necessary to be sensitive to the needs of nesting seabirds; going ashore is not permitted from April 1 to August 31. The lighthouse is not open to the public.

Latitude: 43° 53' 30" N
Longitude: 69° 22' 30" W

**Contact Information:**
**U.S. Fish and Wildlife Service**
**Petit Manan National Wildlife Refuge**
**P.O. Box 279**
**Milbridge, ME 04658**
**(207) 546-2124**
**http://petitmanan.fws.gov/**

# Goat Island Light

Marking the entrance to Cape Porpoise Harbor, Goat Island Light is located on the south end of Goat Island, not far from Kennebunkport, one of New England's earliest settlements. A 20-foot stone tower was originally built for $6,000 in 1835 by order of President Jackson; the beacon was replaced in 1859 with a 25-foot brick tower with a fifth-order Fresnel lens. The current optic is a 300-mm that was installed in 1990, when the light was automated. It shines at 38 feet above sea level for a range of 12 miles and flashes white every 6 seconds.

The second-to-last automated light in the country, Goat Island Light was manned by a traditional lighthouse family until 1990. It is still an active aid to navigation and, because of its proximity to the Bush estate, was also used as a watch point by the U.S. Secret Service during the George H. W. Bush administration.

The original 1860 keeper's quarters still stand, as do the oil house, bath-house, boat launch, and walkway. Goat Island and the light are under the protection of the Kennebunkport Conservation Trust. They were a gift from the U.S. government in 1998.

# Goat Island Light

## Kennebunkport, Maine

### Directions

From I-95, take the Kennebunkport exit and follow Route 35 east to Kennebunk. From there continue east on Route 35/Highway 9A to Kennebunkport. Go left (northeast) on Highway 9 to Cape Porpoise. In Cape Porpoise, turn east onto Pier Road and continue to Bickford Island. The light can be seen on the island to the south. Only distant views are possible from land; the best views are from the water.

Latitude: 43° 21' 30" N
Longitude: 70° 25' 30" W

Contact Information:
Kennebunkport Conservation Trust
P.O. Box 7028
Cape Porpoise, ME 04014
www.thekennebunkportconservation
trust.org

# Goose Rocks Light

Constructed in the "sparkplug" design that was so commonly used in the late 19th century, Goose Rocks Light was built in 1890 to mark the Fox Islands. This design allowed for a two-story integrated keeper's quarters, while its cast-iron construction proved quite sturdy against New England marine weather. In its day, this central location in Penobscot Bay saw quite a lot of ocean traffic.

# Goose Rocks Light

## North Haven, Maine

Originally equipped with a fourth-order Fresnel lens, the light now has a 250-mm, solar-powered lens that flashes red every 4 seconds and has a range of 12 miles. The 51-foot tower is at sea level. It has an integrated foghorn, but since the light is built on a ledge right in the middle of the Fox Islands Thorofare, there is no property on which to construct auxiliary buildings.

## Directions

Goose Rocks Light is best viewed from the water; the station is not open to the public. For lighthouse lovers without personal watercraft, the best option is to take the Maine State Ferry Service to North Haven and take a charter out of North Haven. For more information on the ferry, go to www.state.me.us/mdot/opt/ferry.

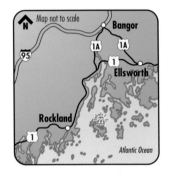

Latitude: 44° 08' 06" N
Longitude: 68° 49' 54" W

Contact Information:
U.S. Coast Guard
Aides to Navigation Team
P.O. Box 5000
Southwest Harbor, ME 04679
www.uscg.mil

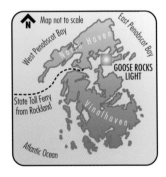

# Great Duck Island Light

Built in 1890 to mark the approach to Blue Hill Bay, 220-acre Great Duck Island Light is named for the thousands of ducks that frequent the large pond in the center of the island.

Owned by the College of the Atlantic, Great Duck Island Light consists of a 42-foot, brick-and-granite tower that shines at 67 feet above sea level. Located 10 miles from Baker Island, the light can be seen for 19 miles. The light's original fifth-order Fresnel lens was replaced in 1986 with a VRB-25 solar-powered aerobeacon that flashes red every 5 seconds. The original 1890 fogbell building still stands, as do the cottage-style keeper's quarters,

**Frenchboro, Maine**

oil house, a storage building, boathouse, and boat ramp. At the turn of the 20th century, a schoolhouse also stood on Great Duck Island to educate the approximately 30 children living on the island, 16 of whom belonged to keeper Nathan Adam Reed.

Great Duck Island is shared by the college, The Nature Conservancy, the State of Maine, and one private resident. Recently renamed the Alice Eno Biological Station, the lighthouse is one of many subjects of research for COA students. For example, the island tractor and boathouse are fueled by biodiesel, an alternative fuel that contains no petroleum, and electricity for the light is generated by a solar array. There is also a biodiesel-powered generator to supplement the solar panels. The lighthouse is now automated and is an active aid to navigation as well as an alternative power demonstration project.

## Directions

The island is not open to the public, and the lighthouse is best viewed by boat. A private hire out of Bar Harbor is the best option for those without their own craft.

Latitude: 44° 08' 30" N
Longitude: 68° 14' 42" W

**Contact Information:**
**College of the Atlantic**
**105 Eden Sreet**
**Bar Harbor, ME 04609**
**(207) 288-5015**
**www.coa.edu**

# Grindle Point Light

Built in 1850 by order of President Pierce, Grindle Point Light is located in Gilkey Harbor in West Penobscot Bay. The beacon was named for Frances Grindel (and is sometimes spelled "Grindel"), who originally owned the property and who became the light's second keeper. Grindle Point Light was rebuilt in 1874 by order of President Grant at the request of mariners who traveled around the area.

One of only six lighthouses in Maine designed with a square tower, it is 39 feet tall. Originally equipped with a fifth-order Fresnel lens, the current 250-mm lens was installed in 1987 and flashes green every 4 seconds with a range of 5 miles. The attached Cape Cod–style keeper's quarters still stand, and they now house the Sailor's Memorial Museum, open in the summer. The 1906 oil house and 1881 boathouse are still standing as well.

In 1934, Grindle Point Light was deactivated and its lantern was housed atop a nearby skeleton tower. The people of Islesboro rallied to have the light reinstated, and in 1987, the lantern was returned to its home in Grindle Point Light and the tower was reinstated as an active aid to navigation.

# Grindle Point Light

## Islesboro, Maine

### Directions

Take the ferry out of Lincolnville east to Grindle Point on Islesboro Island. The lighthouse is right next to the ferry landing.

Latitude: 44° 16' 54" N
Longitude: 68° 56' 36" W

**Contact Information:**
**Town of Islesboro**
**Islesboro, ME 04848**

# Halfway Rock Light

Built on a rocky ledge in Casco Bay off Bailey Island, Halfway Rock Light was approved by President Johnson in 1869 for $50,000, ten times what many lighthouses of the era cost. Even with that amount allocated, because of its precarious location and the fact that the ledge was often submerged, funds ran out and construction stopped. Because the area was heavily trafficked by ships carrying granite and other cargo, however, the pressing need for a lighthouse remained. Construction finally resumed by permission of President Grant. After a delay in the shipment of the third-order Fresnel lens from France, the light was completed in 1871.

Halfway Rock Light was a difficult post. Due to its location, it was often inaccessible during storms. A helicopter landing pad was built on the property in 1961, and the keepers had to be airlifted off the island during a particularly treacherous 1972 squall.

Halfway Rock Light's original Fresnel lens was replaced in 1994 with a VEGA VRB-25 solar-powered optic. The light flashes red every 5 seconds from a 76-foot tower and shines at 77 feet above sea level. It has a range of 19 miles. The light was automated in 1975 and still serves as an active aid to navigation. In 1905, the 1887 fog bell was removed and replaced with a diesel-powered trumpet, which has also since been removed. The 1889 keeper's quarters were destroyed by a storm as were many of the property's other buildings, so only the tower remains.

## Directions

Halfway Rock Light cannot be seen from land and is not open to the public. The lighthouse is 11 miles east of Portland and best viewed by boat or air.

Latitude: 43° 39' 24" N
Longitude: 70° 02' 12" W

**Contact Information:**
American Lighthouse Foundation
P.O. Box 889
Wells, ME 04090
(207) 646-0245
www.lighthousefoundation.org

# Hendricks Head Light

Originally built in 1829, Hendricks Head Light is located on Southport Island at the entrance to the Sheepscot River. The current structure, a square, 39-foot brick tower, was built in 1875 to replace the original whale-oil light lighthouse. The 1875 fifth-order Fresnel lens was in turn replaced in 1979 with a 250-mm optic that shines a fixed light—white to the east and red to the west—at 43 feet above sea level. It has a range of up to 9 miles.

The station was deactivated from 1935 to 1951, when it served only as a day marker. Though privately owned in 1951, the light was relighted by the U.S. Coast Guard in response to marine traffic increases. Today, the 1890 bell tower still stands, though the signal is inactive. The two-story Victorian keeper's quarters remain, as do two cisterns, an 1895 oil house, a garage, a storage building, a catwalk, and an 1880 barn.

Hendricks Head Light is perhaps most famous as the setting for a well-known area fable. According to legend, in the midst of a terrible gale during the 1870s, the keeper of the station sighted a ship washed ashore on a nearby ledge. Unable to reach the ship to assist in the rescue, the keeper and his wife lit a bonfire and kept watch for any survivors who might make their

# Hendricks Head Light

## West Southport, Maine

way to shore. Though no survivors arrived, the keeper rescued a bundle of feather beds tied together that had been thrown overboard from the ship. When he opened the bundle, the keeper discovered a baby girl in a chest with a note entrusting the baby to the care of God. The keeper and his wife, who had recently lost a child, supposedly adopted the girl, whom they named Seaborne, and raised her as their own at the lighthouse.

## Directions

From Wiscasset, take Highway 1 north across the Sheepscot River. Go south on Route 27 to Boothbay Harbor, about 12 miles. Continue on Route 27 south to Southport. Follow Highway 27 south for 13.3 miles where you will cross onto Southport Island, and then continue on Highway 27 for roughly 2 miles to West Southport. In West Southport, turn right on Dogfish Head Road and then left on Beach Road. Follow this to West Southport Beach where you can see the lighthouse to the west. The lighthouse and grounds are not open to the public.

Latitude: 43° 49' 24" N
Longitude: 69° 41' 24" W

**Contact Information:**
Ben Russell
2544 Willow Point Road
Alexander City, AL 35010
www.benrussell.com

# Heron Neck Light

Heron Neck Light was built on Greens Island in 1854 to mark Carver's Harbor on the east side of the south entrance to West Penobscot Bay, an area busy with fishing and lobstering vessels.

Perched on a granite cliff, the 30-foot tower shines a continuous red light at 92 feet above sea level for a range of up to 13 miles. The original fifth-order Fresnel lens was replaced with a 300-mm optic in 1982, the same year the station was automated. The original 1944 foghorn building still stands, as do a 1903 oil house and a generator building.

In 1895 the original keeper's quarters had to be replaced. Then, in 1989, those quarters were badly damaged in a fire. The Island Institute, which owned the property, leased it to a private party who completely refurbished the quarters. It was Heron Neck Light that prompted the Island Institute's Maine Lights Program, which has transferred ownership rights for 28 lighthouses (at this printing) to groups or individuals who vow to restore and preserve the beacons.

# Heron Neck Light

## Vinalhaven, Maine

### Directions

Because you cannot drive to Greens Island from the town of Vinalhaven, Heron Neck Light is best seen by boat. Private charters are available out of Vinalhaven, but keep in mind that the lighthouse is leased to a private individual and is private property.

Latitude: 44° 01' 30"N
Longitude: 68° 51' 42" W

Contact Information:
Island Institute
386 Main Street
Rockland, ME 04841
(207) 594-9209
www.islandinstitute.org

# Indian Island Light

In 1849, the U.S. government purchased Indian Island Light for just $25 for the purpose of building a light station to mark the entrance to Rockport Harbor. The completed beacon, which took the form of a simple keeper's building with a lantern on top, was finished in 1850. Six years later the lantern was replaced by a fourth-order Fresnel lens. The light was deactivated in 1859, but in 1874 the square brick-tower lighthouse that you see today was built.

The lighthouse was deactivated again in 1934, this time permanently. The original 1850 T-shaped keeper's quarters still stand, as do a 1904 oil house, an 1888 fuel house, and two storage buildings.

# Indian Island Light

## Rockport, Maine

### Directions

Located on Indian Island at the entrance to Rockport Harbor, Indian Island Light is privately owned and not open to the public. It can be viewed by boat; private charters are available out of Camden.

Latitude: 44° 09' 56" N
Longitude: 69° 03' 40" W

**Contact Information:**
**Privately owned.**

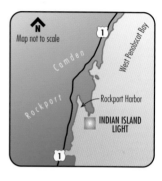

# Isle au Haut Light

Built on Robinson Point on Isle au Haut in East Penobscot Bay, Isle au Haut Light is actually a short distance from shore and is connected to the rest of the property by a dock. The light, the last traditional lighthouse built in Maine, was constructed in 1907 to mark the Isle au Haut Thorofare. The conical, 40-foot-tall tower stands at 48 feet above sea level and its red flash can be seen for up to 8 miles at 4-second intervals. The original fourth-order Fresnel lens was eventually replaced with a 250-mm solar-powered optic, and the station was automated in 1934.

The Victorian keeper's quarters were built in 1907, as were the oil house, boathouse, catwalk, and outhouse, all of which remain. There are also a shed, generator house, storage building, and marine railway on the property.

Now known as the Keeper's House Inn, the facility has no outside electricity or telephones. The inn is run by solar power and the owners invite guests to enjoy the natural beauty of the area, which is located on a small section of Acadia National Park.

# Isle au Haut Light

**Isle au Haut, Maine**

### Directions

Take the mailboat out of Stonington directly to the inn's dock. The lighthouse itself is not open to the public.

Latitude: 44° 03' 54" N
Longitude: 68° 39' 06" W

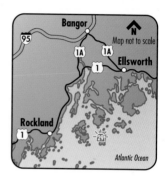

**Contact Information:**
Jeff and Judi Burke
The Keeper's House
P.O. Box 26
Isle au Haut, ME 04645
(207) 367-2261
www.keepershouse.com

# Kennebec River Range Lights

Not to be confused with nearby Doubling Point Light, Doubling Point (also known as Kennebec River) Range Lights are of similar design, and were built for the same reason as Doubling Point: to help mariners make their way up the beautiful but winding Kennebec River. The only set of range lights in Maine, they are set 235 yards apart.

Established in 1898, the Kennebec River Range Lights are 13-foot towers constructed of wood, with the rear tower sporting red trim. On August 6, 1938, these lights were the site of tragedy when keeper William H. Woodward's 10-year-old daughter, Lucy Mae Woodward, apparently drowned while playing in waist-deep water in front of the lights.

In 1980 the original fifth-order Fresnel lenses were replaced with 250-mm optics. The front light shines at 18 feet above sea level and the rear light at 33 feet above sea level. The front light is a quick-flashing white; the rear flashes white at 3-second intervals.

# Kennebec River Range Lights

## Also known as Doubling Point Range Lights
### Arrowsic, Maine

Among the last lights in the country to be automated, the Kennebec River Range Lights were manned until 1990. In 1998, a group of citizens billing themselves as the Range Light Keepers acquired the lights through the Maine Lights Program. Since then, the preservation group has also obtained the lights' fog signal (located a half mile away) and bell tower. The keeper's quarters, oil house, boathouse, fuel house, and a walkway through the marsh also still stand on the property. In addition to restoring these historic structures, the Range Light Keepers have partnered with the Maine Maritime Museum to educate visitors on the history and importance of the landmarks.

The Kennebec River Range Lights are active aids to navigation.

## Directions

The Kennebec River Range Lights can best be seen by boat. Charters are available out of Bath. The lights are not open to the public.

Latitude: (Front) 43° 53' 00" N;
(Rear) 235 yds., 359° from front light
Longitude: (Front) 69° 47' 42" W

**Contact Information:**
Range Light Keepers
79 Iron Mine Road
Arrowsic, ME 04530
(207) 442-7443
www.rlk.org

# Ladies Delight Light

Named for the island reef it marks, Ladies Delight Light is located in Lake Cobbosseecontee in Manchester. Once one of three lights on the lake, this station is now the only freshwater lighthouse in Maine.

Ladies Delight was built in 1908 by the Cobbosseecontee Yacht Club in support of a passenger boat that transported vacationers to destinations on the lake. Because it took about five hours to get around the 9-mile-long lake, and because there were no restroom facilities on the boat, the stop at

# Ladies Delight Light

## Lake Cobbosseecontee, Manchester, Maine

the island provided the female passengers much-needed relief. Consequently, the island was so named.

Standing at 16 feet tall, the tower was originally equipped with a kerosene lamp. It now has a 75-watt bulb with a ship's anchor light lens and is powered by an electric cable out of Manchester.

### Directions

Located about 1 mile south of Island Park in Manchester, Ladies Delight is best viewed by boat. Commodore Stephens of the Cobbosseecontee Yacht Club offers tours by appointment.

Latitude: N/A
Longitude: N/A

**Contact Information:**
**Cobbosseecontee Yacht Club**
**P.O. Box 17**
**Manchester, ME 04351-0017**
**(207) 622-9409**

# Libby Island Light

Marking the entrance to Machias Bay, Libby Island is comprised of two islands joined by a sandbar. The sandbar is sometimes completely submerged and presents a hazard for vessels that believe it to be a clear passage. Coupled with the dense fog that often shrouds the area, it's no wonder that Libby Island has been the site of several shipwrecks. One such example was the Boston-bound *Princeport*, which washed ashore on the sandbar during an 1892 storm when the captain mistook the gap for the Eastern Passage. The crew, who were found clinging to the bow of the ship, were saved in the nick of time by the light keepers.

The 42-foot white granite tower was built in 1822 by order of President Monroe. It shines at 91 feet above sea level for a range of 18 miles. The original lantern was replaced in 1855 with a fourth-order Fresnel lens. The current optic is a solar-powered VRB-25 that signals with two white flashes every 20 seconds. The original fog bell was replaced with a horn in 1884 and the light was automated in 1974.

Thanks to a restoration in 2000, Maine's third-oldest lighthouse looks very much the same today as it did in the 19th century. During that restoration,

# Libby Island Light

the Coast Guard stripped the tower of paint to reveal the original white granite; a boat landing and a retaining wall were also repaired. The original keeper's quarters, which housed three keepers, were dismantled, but there exists an 1893 oil house, generator building, and a fog signal building. The lighthouse is an active aid to navigation.

## Directions

Libby Island can only be reached by boat. If needed, boats can be hired out of Jonesboro, Jonesport, East Machias, or Machiasport. Please keep in mind that because the light is located on a wildlife refuge, it is necessary to be sensitive to the needs of nesting seabirds; going ashore is not permitted from April 1 to August 31. The station is not open to the public.

Latitude: 44° 34' 06" N
Longitude: 67° 22' 00" W

Contact Information:
U.S. Fish and Wildlife Service
Petit Manan National Wildlife Refuge
P.O. Box 279
Milbridge, ME 04658
(207) 546-2124
http://petitmanan.fws.gov/

## Little Mark Island Monument

Built as a daymarker in 1827, Little Mark Island Monument—a neat pyramidal tower of granite blocks marked with a black vertical stripe that denotes the Merriconeag Sound—is not considered a lighthouse in the traditional sense. At 50 feet tall, it stands as high as a lighthouse, and it is maintained as an active aid to navigation by the U.S. Coast Guard; it is not clear when the daymarker was transformed into a lighted beacon. Lighted it is, though, and it shines at 74 feet above sea level for a distance of 5 miles, flashing white every 4 seconds. The station has never had a house or a keeper, though there is a large square room at the base once used to provide shelter for mariners in need; presently, this room is used to store batteries for the structure's lantern.

# Little Mark Island Monument

### Directions

The light is about a mile southwest of Bailey
Island in Casco Bay and is best seen by boat.
Charters are available out of Portland for those
without private boats.

Latitude: 43° 42' 30" N
Longitude: 70° 01' 54" W

**Contact Information:**
**U.S. Coast Guard**
**Aides to Navigation Team**
**P.O. Box 5000**
**Southwest Harbor, ME 04679**
**www.uscg.mil**

# Little River Light

Marking the entrance to Cutler Harbor, Little River Light was built in 1847 by order of President Polk. Located about halfway between Mount Desert and Passamaquoddy Bay, Cutler Harbor was the last protected harbor on the Maine coast before Canada; it remains a busy port for fishermen as well as vacationers. Considered a desirable station for keepers, Little River Light is less than a mile from shore.

The original lantern was replaced in 1855 with a fifth-order Fresnel lens, and then the entire lantern portion of the old lighthouse was moved to a new tower in 1876. The 1876 tower is 41 feet high and constructed of cast iron and brick. The station was automated in 1974 and replaced by a skeletal tower in 1975. Its VRB-25 aerobeacon flashes white every 6 seconds and shines at 56 feet above sea level for a range of 13 miles. The original bell tower has been dismantled, but the 1888 Victorian-style keeper's quarters still stand.

The first New England lighthouse to have its ownership transferred under the National Historic Lighthouse Preservation Act of 2000, Little River Light is now leased by the American Lighthouse Foundation. In 2001, after

# Little River Light

**Cutler, Maine**

27 years in darkness and just 3 years after being placed on the state's most endangered properties list, Little River Light was relighted. Restoration efforts are ongoing by the American Lighthouse Foundation, which sponsors periods during which the general public can lend a helping hand.

## Directions

Because it is located on the far side of Little River Island, Little River Light must be seen by boat; charters are available out of Cutler. The station is not open to the public.

Latitude: 44° 39' 06" N
Longitude: 67° 11' 30" W

**Contact Information:**
American Lighthouse Foundation
P.O. Box 889
Wells, ME 04090
(207) 646-0245
www.lighthousefoundation.org

# Lubec Channel Light

Marking the western entrance to the town of Lubec, Lubec Channel Light is a sparkplug-style light surrounded by water on a rock foundation. Ordered in 1890 by President Harrison, this was one of the last lighthouses built in Maine; it served the sardine fishing industry important to the area at the time. Once a booming business in Lubec, only two sardine canneries are still operational.

With a tower height of 40 feet, the light flashes white every 6 seconds at 53 feet above sea level. Though the tower comprises five levels, only two were designated as keeper's quarters. Owing to the lack of room for families, the station was considered a "stag" assignment for two male keepers.

The station was automated in 1939, after an unfortunate incident in which a keeper died from inhaling fumes from a defective heater. There was once a fog bell at the site, then later a foghorn. The original fourth-order Fresnel lens was replaced in 1985 by a 155-mm solar-powered lens.

Lubec Channel Light was scheduled to be discontinued and abandoned by the Coast Guard in 1989. However, an extensive local campaign dubbed

# Lubec Channel Light

"Save the Sparkplug" got underway. Local enthusiasts even handed out automobile sparkplugs to gain attention for the cause. Their mission was a success, and in 1992 the Coast Guard began a $700,000 restoration of Lubec Channel Light. Today, the lighthouse is fully stabilized and sports a fresh coat of paint. Though it still has a bit of a tilt, it is an active aid to navigation.

## Directions

From Route 1 in Whiting, travel east on Highway 189 about 10 miles toward Lubec. Turn south on Lubec Road and follow to the beach. During low tide, it is possible to walk out to the lighthouse, but this is not recommended because the tides come in very fast and high and could leave visitors stranded. The station is not open to the public.

Latitude: 44° 50' 30" N
Longitude: 66° 58' 36" W

Contact Information:
U.S. Coast Guard
Aides to Navigation Team
P.O. Box 5000
Southwest Harbor, ME 04679
www.uscg.mil

# Marshall Point Light

Marking the entrance to Port Clyde Harbor, Marshall Point station was established in 1832 as an aid to mariners serving the busy fishing and granite industries. The first stone building was replaced in 1857 with the granite tower seen today. Because of its location on a peninsula, the area was also a militarily strategic spot for 17th- and 18th-century settlers seeking distance from Native Americans.

In the 20th century, the area became popular as a haven for artists, including Andrew Wyeth and his son, Jamie. Indeed, on any given day, you're likely to find smatterings of artists behind easels or tripods looking to capture the photogenic beauty of Marshall Point Light. The station has even been featured on the big screen: it was the finishing point for Tom Hanks's cross-country run in the film *Forrest Gump*.

The 1857, 31-foot tower was originally equipped with a fifth-order Fresnel lens. In 1981, shortly after the station was automated, the Fresnel lens was replaced with a 300-mm optic that can be seen for 7 miles and shines a fixed white light. The striking colonial revival–style keeper's quarters were built in 1895 and restored by the St. George Historical Society in 1990. The dwelling

# Marshall Point Light

now houses a museum on the first floor; the second floor is rented out to tenants. The 1898 oil house still stands, but the bell tower built that year has been dismantled. The property is owned by the town of St. George, which acquired the landmarks through the Maine Lights Program in 1998. The grounds are open to the public all year; the lighthouse museum is open from May to October.

## Directions

From U.S. Route 1 just north of Thomaston Village, take Maine Route 131 south through St. George and Tenants Harbor to Port Clyde. Turn left just beyond the Ocean House in Port Clyde at the Marshall Point Museum sign (Factory Road). Continue to a "T" intersection at Marshall Point Road. Turn right onto Marshall Point Road and follow the road between two stone pillars. The road narrows and ends at the parking area for the lighthouse and museum.

Latitude: 43° 55' 00" N
Longitude: 69° 15' 42" W

**Contact Information:**
**Marshall Point Lighthouse Museum**
**Marshall Point Road**
**P.O. Box 247**
**Port Clyde, ME 04855**
**(207) 372-6450**
**www.marshallpoint.org**

# Matinicus Rock Light

Established in 1827 by order of President John Quincy Adams, Matinicus Rock Light is located on the isolated Matinicus Rock, a 30-acre ledge 22 miles out from the entrance to Penobscot Bay. The farthest lighthouse from the Maine coast, the desolate island was vulnerable to violent storms and is the source of many romantic lighthouse tales.

One of the most famous is that of Abbie Burgess, daughter of keeper Samuel Burgess. Because Samuel's son was frequently off on fishing trips and Samuel's wife was an invalid, Abbie was assigned the duty of assisting her father in keeping the twin lights going. Once a month, Abbie cared for her mother and sisters while her father sailed the 26 miles to Rockland to obtain supplies. Unfortunately, in 1856, one of the biggest storms in Maine's history occurred while keeper Burgess was on the mainland. In addition to tending the lights from dusk to dawn for four straight weeks, Abbie cared for her three sisters and sick mother and even saved their lives by moving the family to the beacon's north tower; the keeper's quarters were washed away shortly thereafter. Abbie continued to serve lighthouses in the capacity of keeper for the majority of her life, and upon her deathbed expressed in a letter to a friend: "If I ever have a gravestone, I would like it in the form of a light-

# Matinicus Rock Light

### Criehaven, Maine

house or beacon." In 1945, her wish came true when an aluminum scale replica of a lighthouse was placed at her gravesite.

The first station at Matinicus Rock consisted of two wooden towers, which were rebuilt in 1846 with the addition of a granite keeper's quarters. In 1857, they were rebuilt again—as seen today—180 feet apart so they would be effective range lights. One tower was deactivated in 1924, but the other stands 48 feet high and shines at 90 feet above sea level. With a range of 20 miles, the station was automated in 1983. In 1993 the third-order Fresnel lens installed on the 1857 tower was replaced with a VEGA VRB-25 solar-powered aerobeacon that flashes white every 10 seconds.

## Directions

Located on Matinicus Rock, 26 miles south of shore, Matinicus Rock Light can only be viewed by boat; charters are available out of Vinalhaven and a ferry is available to Matinicus Isle. Please keep in mind that because the light is located on a wildlife refuge, it is necessary to be sensitive to the needs of nesting seabirds; going ashore is not permitted from April 1 to August 31.

Latitude: 43° 47' 00" N
Longitude: 68° 51' 18" W

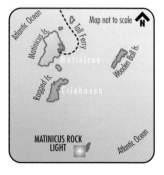

**Contact Information:**
**U.S. Fish and Wildlife Service**
**Petit Manan National Wildlife Refuge**
**P.O. Box 279**
**Milbridge, ME 04658**
**(207) 546-2124**
**http://petitmanan.fws.gov/**

# Monhegan Island Light

The landing site for such explorers as Weymouth, Champlain, and John Smith, Monhegan Island (a Native American name meaning "Island of the Sea") is located 10 miles off the Maine coast, but stood out to explorers in search of the New World. For the same reason, it was a natural place to build a lighthouse to serve the fishing industry and tradeships in 1824.

The first tower was a 30-foot cobblestone structure that was dismantled in 1850 when the existing 47-foot lighthouse was built. Shining at 178 feet above sea level, the light has a range of 20 miles. In 1853, the Lighthouse Board stated in its report that "there should be a bell at Monhegan. The light-house is so far from the point where the bell should be situated, that the light-keeper could not attend to it, and it will be advisable, therefore, to have a house built on which the bell might be placed; and a man should be appointed

# Monhegan Island Light

## Monhegan, Maine

whose sole duty should be to take charge of the bell. The proper site for the bell is on a small island which lies off Monhegan, called Manana. For the house and bell, and for purchasing the land, the sum of $3,500 will be necessary."

In 1866, Congress approved funding for the project, and in 1876, the fog signal for Monhegan Island Light was officially relocated to Manana Island. Approximately 10 years later, a system was installed that allowed the keeper at Monhegan to ring a gong in the bedroom of the Manana station to alert that keeper that fog was rolling in.

Automated in 1959, the station is now equipped with a VEGA VRB-25 solar-powered aerobeacon that flashes white every 15 seconds. The keeper's quarters, built in 1874, still stand. The Monhegan Historical and Cultural Museum Association has rebuilt the 1857 assistant keeper's quarters to house a museum with exhibits on local history and industry, and art from local artists. Edward Hopper, Rockwell Kent, George Bellows, and the Wyeths are among those who have been featured in the museum, which is open summers only.

## Directions

Monhegan Island Light is on Monhegan Island, to which ferries are available out of Port Clyde, New Harbor, and Boothbay Harbor.

Latitude: 43° 45' 54" N
Longitude: 69° 18' 54" W

Contact Information:
Monhegan Historical and
Cultural Museum Association
1 Lighthouse Hill
Monhegan, ME 04852
(207) 596-7003
www.monheganmuseum.org

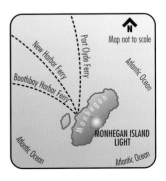

# Moose Peak Light

Located on the eastern point of rocky Mistake Island, Moose Peak Light station was established in 1827 by order of John Quincy Adams. Situated in an area vulnerable to fog, the station was built to serve the fishing and freight industries, warning of the many shoals from Moose Peak Light to Mark Island and into Jonesport. In the early 20th century, Moose Peak Light experienced more fog than any other station, logging foggy conditions over 1,600 hours per year. At one point, the foghorn sounded for 181 consecutive hours.

The existing 57-foot tower was first lighted in 1851, but the second-order Fresnel lens installed in 1856 was replaced with a DCB-24 rotating optic in 1993. Automated in 1972, the light shines at 72 feet above sea level, flashing white every 30 seconds for a range of 20 miles. The often-used foghorn building, built in 1912, still exists, but the 1903 keeper's quarters were demolished in a 1982 military exercise. As a result of errors during this exercise, the lighthouse was slightly damaged as well.

Still an active aid to navigation, the property is leased by the U.S. Coast Guard to The Nature Conservancy.

# Moose Peak Light

### Directions

Moose Peak Light, located on Mistake Island south of Jonesport, is best viewed by boat; a charter can be taken out of Jonesport. The lighthouse is not open to the public.

Latitude: 44° 28' 30" N
Longitude: 67° 31' 54" W

**Contact Information:**
**U.S. Coast Guard**
**Aides to Navigation Team**
**P.O. Box 5000**
**Southwest Harbor, ME 04679**
**www.uscg.mil**

# Mount Desert Rock Light

Located 26 miles from the mainland, Mount Desert Rock is a rocky ledge situated 22 miles from Mount Desert Island and hosts one of the most storm-battered and isolated light stations in the nation. Named by Samuel de Champlain in 1604, the island has been, not surprisingly, the site of many shipwrecks. One famous wreck was that of the tugboat *Astral*, which ran into Mount Desert Rock in December 1902. Seventeen of its 18 crewmembers survived, thanks to the efforts of the keeper and his wife, who, despite sub-zero temperatures, were able to bring them ashore with a line and save them from freezing.

Though many legends surrounding Mount Desert Rock Light are dismal, there is at least one uplifting anecdote as well. In the 1850s, a keeper brought his wife soil and some seeds, which she planted in crevices around

# Mount Desert Rock Light

## Mount Desert Rock, Maine

the rock. Passing sailors began to refer to the garden as "God's Rock Garden," and for several years they brought soil and flowers to the keepers to prolong the tradition.

Established in 1830, the station originally consisted of a wooden tower that stood 56 feet above the ocean on top of stone keeper's quarters. The existing 58-foot granite tower was built in 1847 and equipped with a third-order Fresnel lens in 1858. In 1993, a VEGA VRG-25 solar-powered optic was installed. Shining at 75 feet above sea level, the light has a range of 20 miles and flashes white every 15 seconds. The fog signal building has been removed, but the 1892 keeper's quarters, cistern, storage building, and boathouse still stand.

The station was automated in 1977 and remains an active aid to navigation. Mount Desert Rock is owned by the College of the Atlantic and is used primarily as a whale research station.

## Directions

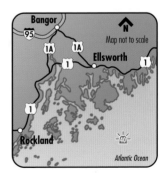

Mount Desert Rock is not open to the public; the lighthouse is best viewed by boat. Charters are available out of Bar Harbor.

Latitude: 43° 58' 06" N
Longitude: 68° 07' 42" W

Contact Information:
College of the Atlantic
105 Eden Street
Bar Harbor, ME 04609
(207) 288-5015
www.coa.edu

# Narraguagus Island Light

Narraguagus (or Pond) Island Light is located on the east side of Pond Island, on the west side of Narraguagus Bay near Milbridge. Built in 1853 by order of President Pierce, the 31-foot tower was initially constructed to serve the fishing and lumber industries. Before being purchased by the U.S. government, the three acres on which the station stands were privately owned and used for farming.

Shortly after the lighthouse was constructed, an inn was built on the island. A clubhouse and golf course were soon added and the area became something of a resort destination.

Deactivated in 1934, Narraguagus Island Light is now under private ownership. The 1875 keeper's quarters remain, as do two storage buildings, an oil house, and a brick workroom that links the tower with the quarters. The light is still useful as a daymark to passing vessels.

# Narraguagus Island Light

### Also known as Pond Island Light
### Milbridge, Maine

## Directions

Narraguagus Island Light is best viewed by boat. Charters are available out of Milbridge or Winter Harbor. The lighthouse is not open to the public.

Latitude: 44° 27' 12" N
Longitude: 67° 49' 56" W

## Contact Information:
## Privately owned.

# Nash Island Light

Marking the entrance to Pleasant and Harrington Bays, Nash Island Light was established in 1838 by order of President Van Buren. In 1874, under President Grant, the station was rebuilt to mark the shoals around the island—particularly those that lie between Nash Island and Petit Manan—all the way to Tabbett's Narrows.

The original tower was made of stone and had a lamp reflector until a Fresnel lens was installed in 1856. The existing 29-foot square tower was originally equipped with a fourth-order Fresnel lens, which shone at a height of 57 feet.

# Nash Island Light

## South Addison, Maine

As a family station, many of the keepers at Nash Island had children, and schooling became an issue. At one point, a school was run on the island with a teacher from the mainland. Jenny Cirone, daughter of keeper John Purington, who tended to the lighthouse from 1916 to 1935, has been quoted as saying, "We started out havin' a teacher out there on the island. And we'd get in, well maybe, possibly four weeks out of the year. This teacher'd go from island to island, two weeks here, two weeks there. By the time she got back to our island, we'd already forgot what she'd learned us. Then she'd go home and one of my brothers'd propose. That's what kept happenin' to 'em. My seven brothers took to marryin' 'em as fast as they come on the island."

Jenny Cirone remained on Nash Island for the majority of her life and became one of the area's most well-liked and influential residents. Spurred on by her memory, the Friends of Nash Island Light are working to preserve the deactivated light station. Nash Island itself is now a refuge for eider, herring gulls, and black-backed gulls, and Jenny Cirone's sheep can be found there, as well.

## Directions

Nash Island Light is best seen by boat; charters are available out of South Addison and Cape Split Harbor. Please keep in mind that because the light is located on a wildlife refuge, it is necessary to be sensitive to the needs of nesting seabirds; going ashore is not permitted from April 1 to August 31. The lighthouse is not open to the public.

Latitude: 44° 27' 51" N
Longitude: 67° 44' 50" N

Contact Information:
Friends of Nash Island Light
P.O. Box 250
Addison, ME 04606

# Owls Head Light

Located in West Penobscot Bay, Owls Head Light is located on Owls Head, a rocky headland south of Rockland. Owls Head is named for formations on the headland that are said to resemble the eyes and nose of an owl. The current light is the same one built in 1826 by order of President John Quincy Adams to serve the lime and freight industries.

The 30-foot brick tower at Owls Head was originally equipped with a lantern system. In 1856 a fourth-order Fresnel lens was installed and still operates, though the light was automated in 1989. Shining a fixed white light at 100 feet above sea level, the light can be seen for 16 miles. The fog signal building and boathouse have been removed, but the 1854 wood-frame, cottage-style keeper's dwelling still stands, as do a generator house, walkway, and oil storage building. The light is an active aid to navigation and the keeper's quarters house U.S. Coast Guard personnel.

# Owls Head Light

In addition to being one of Maine's most striking light stations, Owls Head Light is also one of the most lore-steeped. One of the most notable legends is that of the "frozen lovers." According to the tale, one of three passengers on a shipwrecked schooner managed to escape from a blanket of ice that covered the ship and stumbled to the road leading to Owls Head Light. There, he was spotted and rescued by the station's keeper. He told the keeper about the two other passengers, an engaged couple. By the time a rescue crew arrived, the couple was found in an embrace, frozen in a block of ice. Though they appeared to be dead, the keeper brought them back to the station, where they recovered; the couple eventually married.

Another story from Owls Head chronicles the skills of Spot, a springer spaniel who lived at the lighthouse in the 1930s. The dog learned how to pull the rope that triggered the fog bell. One particularly stormy night, the fog bell froze. It is said that Spot saved the Matinicus mailboat from crashing into Owls Head that night by warning the ship's captain of the island's location with his loud barks.

## Directions

From Rockland, take Route 73 south. Turn left on North Shore Road and follow the signs to the lighthouse.

Latitude: 44° 05' 30" N
Longitude: 69° 02' 36" W

Contact Information:
U.S. Coast Guard
Aides to Navigation Team
P.O. Box 5000
Southwest Harbor, ME 04679
www.uscg.mil

# Pemaquid Point Light

One of the early light stations established on the Maine coast, Pemaquid Point Light was built in 1827 for $4,000. Perched on the edge of a rocky granite promontory along Muscongus Bay, the light was erected to serve the fishing and lumber industries. Because of its age and classic looks, Pemaquid Point is featured on the Maine quarter of the U.S. Mint's 50 State Quarters Program.

Just eight years after its construction, the crumbling original tower was replaced with a new white rubblestone tower. The 10 lanterns that were moved to that tower were replaced in 1856 with a fourth-order Fresnel lens. The first lighthouse in Maine to be automated, in 1934, Pemaquid Point Light is still an active aid to navigation. The 38-foot tower rises 79 feet above sea level and the light has a range of 14 miles, flashing white every 6 seconds.

The Cape Cod–style keeper's quarters still stand and serve as a Fishermen's Museum. The lens from the Baker Island Light is on display at the museum, as are photographs and displays of the area's fishing industry in an adjoining art gallery. The surrounding property has been made into a park and Easter Sunday sunrise services are a popular annual event at the site. A 1992 sound signal building replaced the 1897 structure, which was destroyed in a storm. There is also an oil house on the property.

# Pemaquid Point Light

**Bristol, Maine**

Today, Pemaquid Point Light is leased by the American Lighthouse Foundation, which has established a chapter called the Friends of Pemaquid Point Lighthouse to manage the tower.

## Directions

From Bristol, take Route 130 south all the way to Pemaquid Point.

Latitude: 43° 50' 12" N
Longitude: 69° 30' 24" W

**Contact Information:**
American Lighthouse Foundation
P.O. Box 889
Wells, ME 04090
(207) 646-0245
www.lighthousefoundation.org

# Perkins Island Light

Located on rocky Perkins Island on the east side of the Kennebec River, Perkins Island Light was built in 1898 in support of Bath's shipbuilding industry. The first U.S. Navy ships built in Bath in 1862 were part of a tradition of shipbuilding and repair in the Bath area that continues today.

The 23-foot octagonal wooden tower was originally equipped with a fifth-order Fresnel lens. In 1979 a 250-mm lens was installed that flashes red every 2.5 seconds at 41 feet above sea level, for a range of 6 miles. Automated in 1959, Perkins Island Light is an active aid to navigation and is owned by the U.S. Coast Guard. The other structures and property surrounding the lighthouse are owned by the State of Maine and used as a park.

In 2000, Perkins Island Light was added to *Lighthouse Digest*'s Doomsday List; that same year, the American Lighthouse Foundation leased the lighthouse from the Coast Guard and established a chapter called Friends of Perkins Island Lighthouse. The group hopes to construct a replica of the 1901 boathouse and a ramp and eventually reconstruct the badly damaged original Victorian keeper's quarters. Other buildings still standing at the site are the recently restored pyramid-shaped fog bell tower built in 1902, a 1906 oil house, and the 1898 barn.

# Perkins Island Light

## Georgetown, Maine

### Directions

Perkins Island is located in the Kennebec River just west of Georgetown. There are no roads to Perkins Island, but private charters are available out of Bath for those without their own boat.

Latitude: 43° 47' 12" N
Longitude: 69° 47' 06" W

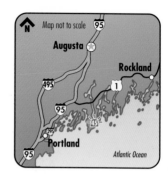

**Contact Information:**
American Lighthouse Foundation
P.O. Box 889
Wells, ME 04090
(207) 646-0245
www.lighthousefoundation.org

# Petit Manan Light

Built on Petit Manan Island, located in the Atlantic Ocean between Narraguagus and Frenchman Bays, Petit Manan Light marks the island and the reef that connects it to the mainland at Petit Manan Point. Weather conditions were difficult when the light was first established in 1817, and soon after, living conditions became so bad that the station's first keeper left his post to the care of his wife. Mrs. Jeremiah Leighton may have been the nation's first female lighthouse keeper, serving until 1831.

Although living conditions improved over the years, a new tower was built in 1855. At 119 feet, this granite-and-brick tower is a very tall lighthouse for its generation. It was originally equipped with a second-order Fresnel lens, but has since been updated to a VRB-25 solar-powered optic that flashes white every 10 seconds at 123 feet above sea level for a range of 19 miles. Automated in 1972, this station is an active aid to navigation.

# Petit Manan Light

## Milbridge, Maine

The keeper's quarters dating from 1875 still stand, as do the 1887 foghorn building, engine house, rain shed, boathouse, boardwalk, boat ramp, helipad, outhouse, and oil house. The surrounding property is a national wildlife refuge where puffins are a big attraction. As of summer 2004, Petit Manan Light has been available for stewardship through the National Historic Preservation Act of 2000. If no applicable steward is found, the lighthouse may be sold.

## Directions

Located on Petit Manan Island, Petit Manan Light can be seen distantly from Petit Manan Point, but is best seen by boat. A boat can be hired out of Milbridge or Bar Harbor. Please keep in mind that because the light is located on a wildlife refuge, it is necessary to be sensitive to the needs of nesting seabirds; going ashore is not permitted from April 1 to August 31.

Latitude: 44° 22' 06" N
Longitude: 67° 51' 54" W

**Contact Information:**
**U.S. Coast Guard**
**Aides to Navigation Team**
**P.O. Box 5000**
**Southwest Harbor, ME 04679**
**www.uscg.mil**

**U.S. Fish and Wildlife Service**
**Petit Manan National Wildlife Refuge**
**P.O. Box 279**
**Milbridge, ME 04658**
**(207) 546-2124**
**http://petitmanan.fws.gov/**

# Pond Island Light

Not to be confused with Narraguagus Island Light in Milbridge, which is also sometimes referred to as Pond Island Light, this beacon marks the west side of the entrance to the Kennebec River near Popham Beach. Pond Island Light was established in 1821 with an integrated tower and quarters on 10-acre Pond Island. A 20-foot cylindrical brick tower that stands at 52 feet above sea level replaced the original structure in 1855. Originally equipped with a fifth-order Fresnel lens, a 250-mm optic has since been installed, offering a range of 9 miles and flashing a white light for 3 seconds on, 3 seconds off. Automated in 1963, Pond Island Light is an active aid to navigation.

The fog bell building was destroyed in 1869, and the 1855 Cape Cod–style keeper's quarters were removed in 1963.

Used as a station for soldiers during the War of 1812 and as a stopover for steamships, Pond Island is now part of the Petit Manan National Wildlife Refuge and is home to a number of nesting terns, common eiders, and a variety of shorebirds and songbirds.

# Pond Island Light

## Directions

From Highway 1 in Bath, go south on 209 all the way to Popham Beach State Park. For a closer look, charter boats to Pond Island are available out of Atkins Bay. Please keep in mind that because the light is located on a wildlife refuge, it is necessary to be sensitive to the needs of nesting seabirds; going ashore is not permitted from April 1 to August 31.

Latitude: 43° 44' 24" N
Longitude: 69° 46' 12" W

**Contact Information:**
**U.S. Fish and Wildlife Service**
**Petit Manan National Wildlife Refuge**
**P.O. Box 279**
**Milbridge, ME 04658**
**(207) 546-2124**
**http://petitmanan.fws.gov/**

# Portland Breakwater Light

Located just off the coast of South Portland, Portland Breakwater Light marks the coast for mariners in Casco Bay. Built in 1875, the current light-house replaced the original 1855 structure that was built as part of the large Portland Breakwater that protects the harbor against the damaging storms of the Atlantic Ocean.

Built to resemble the Choragic Monument of Lysicrates, a fourth-century Greek monument, the tower has six Corinthian columns built into the sides that distinguish it from other lighthouse towers. The 1875 light was equipped with a sixth-order Fresnel lens that has since been removed. The light was automated in 1934, when the original 1889 keeper's quarters were removed; the keeper from nearby Spring Point Ledge Light was then assigned the double duty of tending to both the Spring Point Ledge and Portland Breakwater stations. Portland Breakwater Light was deactivated all together in 1942 when the government filled in the breakwater to provide dry docks during World War II.

# Portland Breakwater Light

## Also known as Bug Light
## South Portland, Maine

The Maine Historical Preservation Committee began to raise funds in 1989 for an eventual restoration that included a new coat of paint and structural repairs. In 2002, the work on the lighthouse was completed and the beacon was relighted on August 14, 2002, with a 250-mm optic that flashes white every 4 seconds. A public park is adjacent to Portland Breakwater Light.

### Directions

From I-95, take exit 7 and go straight off the ramp to Route 1 (Main Street). Turn north (left) on Route 1 and follow to Broadway. Bear right on Broadway but stay left. Follow Broadway past the entrance to the bridge to Portland on the left, but continue on Broadway going right. Follow Broadway to the end and turn left on Breakwater Drive. Turn right on Madison Street and follow it to the end, where you will find Breakwater Park.

Latitude: 43° 39' 20" N
Longitude: 70° 14' 05" W

**Contact Information:**
**City of South Portland**
**25 Cottage Road**
**South Portland, ME 04106**
**(207) 767-3201**
**www.southportland.org**

# Portland Head Light

One of only four remaining lighthouses built by order of President Washington, Portland Head Light marks Portland Harbor on Casco Bay. The station was originally ordered by the General Court of Massachusetts in 1787, which provided $750 for construction of the beacon; when the U.S. government gained control of all lighthouses in 1790, an additional $1,500 was granted for its completion. Constructed of rubblestone with a brick lining, the light took four years to build.

Heightened in 1864 after the wreck of the British vessel *Bohemian*, in which 40 immigrants died, the tower was raised 20 feet and its fourth-order Fresnel lens was replaced with a second-order version. Portland Head Light's 80-foot conical tower now shines at 101 feet above sea level for a range of 24 miles. The station was automated in 1989 and a DCB-224 aerobeacon was installed in 1991 that flashes white every 4 seconds.

In 1975 a replica of the 1880 foghorn building was constructed. It still stands, as do a garage and oil house. The Museum at Portland Head Light now occupies the former keeper's quarters. Also located nearby is a rock inscribed: IN MEMORY OF THE SHIP ANNIE C. MAGUIRE, WRECKED HERE, DEC. 24, 1886.

# Portland Head Light

## Cape Elizabeth, Maine

The 14 people aboard the ship were rescued by the keeper and his family, but the ship was destroyed in a storm days later.

Author Henry Wadsworth Longfellow was a frequent visitor to Portland Head Light in its early days; in fact, it is said that his poem, "The Lighthouse," was inspired by the romantic beacon.

An active aid to navigation, the station is owned by the Town of Cape Elizabeth, which grants the U.S. Coast Guard access to the optic and sound signal.

## Directions

From 295 in Portland, take Route 77 south to South Portland. Turn left on Broadway, then right on Cottage Road. Cottage Road becomes Shore Road at the Cape Elizabeth town line. Approaching from the south, take Route 1 north to Oak Hill in Scarborough. Turn right on Route 207, then left on Route 77 north to Cape Elizabeth. Turn right onto Shore Road. Portland Head Light is located in Fort Williams Park.

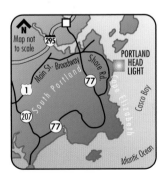

Latitude: 43° 37' 24" N
Longitude: 70° 12' 30" W

**Contact Information:**
**The Museum at Portland Head Light**
**1000 Shore Road**
**Cape Elizabeth, ME 04107**
**(207) 799-2661**
**www.portlandheadlight.com**

# Prospect Harbor Point Light

Prospect Harbor Point Light was built in 1850 on the east side of the harbor entrance in support of area fishing fleets. The original granite structure with an integrated light tower was replaced in 1891 with a more modern, classic revival–style quarters separate from the 38-foot tower. The new station was equipped with a fifth-order Fresnel lens that has since been replaced with a 250-mm optic that flashes red every 6 seconds.

The station was deactivated from 1859 to 1870 because it was determined by the Lighthouse Board that marine activity did not require it. It was relighted in 1870 and automated in 1951.

The 1891 keeper's quarters, known as Gull Cottage, still stand and were renovated in 1969 for recreational use by active and retired navy personnel. The oil house and wooden boat shed also still stand. The other buildings are used by the navy and the lighthouse is an active aid to navigation.

In 2000, Prospect Harbor Point Light was leased by the American Lighthouse Foundation. As of August 2004, the organization is restoring the tower's stairway and lantern and repairing water damage that had occurred from leaks in the tower.

# Prospect Harbor Point Light

**Prospect Harbor, Maine**

### Directions

Prospect Harbor Point Light is located on secure U.S. Navy property; therefore, land access is prohibited and approaching by boat is not recommended. It can be seen from Prospect Harbor along Route 195. The lighthouse is not open to the public.

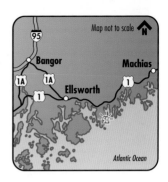

Latitude: 44° 24' 12" N
Longitude: 68° 00' 48" W

**Contact Information:**
**American Lighthouse Foundation**
**P.O. Box 889**
**Wells, ME 04090**
**(207) 646-0245**
**www.lighthousefoundation.org**

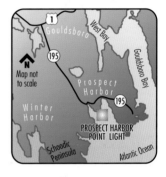

# Pumpkin Island Light

Built in 1854 by order of President Pierce, Pumpkin Island Light marks the entrance to East Penobscot Bay at Eggemoggin Reach. The light was built in support of the lumbering industry and the traffic it created to destinations such as Boston and New York.

Deactivated in 1933 and replaced by a ledge buoy, Pumpkin Island Light was sold at auction in 1934 and has since passed through the hands of several private owners. The station is located on a small island of about an acre. The 28-foot brick tower was equipped with a fifth-order Fresnel lens that shone at 43 feet above sea level. Attached to the tower are the 1854 Cape Cod–style keeper's quarters. A boathouse and an oil house also remain.

# Pumpkin Island Light

## Little Deer Isle, Maine

### Directions

From Orland, take Route 175 south to Route 15. Take Route 15 south to Little Deer Isle. Turn right on Eggemoggin Road and follow it to the end. The lighthouse is just offshore, but is on private property.

Latitude: 44° 18' 33" N
Longitude: 68° 44' 34" W

### Contact Information: Privately owned.

# Ram Island Ledge Light

Not to be confused with Ram Island Light in Fisherman Island Passage, Ram Island Ledge Light is located on the north side of the entrance to Portland Harbor. One of the newer lighthouses in Maine, it was built in 1905 to mark the partially submerged ledge that runs from Ram Island to the harbor. Ram Island Ledge was responsible for many shipwrecks despite the iron spindle placed on the ledge in 1855; it wasn't until the 400-foot transatlantic ship *California* ran aground on the ledge in 1900 that the government decided to establish a light station.

The 72-foot tower is made of granite blocks and stands at 77 feet above sea level for a range of 8 miles. Construction of this lighthouse was particularly difficult, as the location is underwater for all but a few hours per day. A total of 699 four-ton blocks were cut and numbered before leaving the quarry in Vinalhaven so they would be ready for assembly once they arrived at the ledge.

# Ram Island Ledge Light

## Portland, Maine

Originally equipped with a third-order Fresnel lens, Ram Island Ledge Light now operates as an active aid to navigation with a 300-mm solar-powered optic that flashes white twice every 6 seconds. The keeper's quarters are integrated within the tower, but they have not been used as such since the station was automated in 1959.

## Directions

Ram Island Ledge Light is best seen by boat, but can be seen from Portland Head Light. Private charters are available out of Portland or Cape Elizabeth. The station is not open to the public.

Latitude: 43° 37' 54"
Longitude: 70° 11' 12" W

**Contact Information:**
**U.S. Coast Guard**
**Aides to Navigation Team**
**P.O. Box 5000**
**Southwest Harbor, ME 04679**
**www.uscg.mil**

# Ram Island Light

Built in 1883 by order of President Arthur, Ram Island Light is located on Ram Island in Boothbay Harbor's Fisherman Island Passage. Part of a dangerous archipelago comprising Ram Island, Fisherman Island, Outer Heron Island, White Islands, Damariscove Island, and The Hypocrites, the area around Ram Island threatened mariners of the late 19th century. First marked unofficially by lobstering captains and fishermen, there are stories of the island being haunted by the spirits of shipwreck victims.

The 35-foot structure we see today is built of brick and granite. Once equipped with a fourth-order Fresnel, it now has a 250-mm optic that can be seen for 11 miles and flashes red 3 seconds on, 3 seconds off. The Victorian-style foghorn building built in 1883 no longer stands. A cistern, brick oil house, storage building, and barn do remain at the site, though.

Ram Island Light is owned by the Grand Banks Schooner Museum Trust, which saved the lighthouse from being demolished in 1983. The group is successfully restoring the badly run-down light station. Repairs have included adding a new catwalk from the tower to the keeper's quarters; the previous one had been deemed too badly rotted to repair and was demolished by the Coast Guard during a 1977 restoration of the beacon.

The Coast Guard has access to the active navigation aid's optic.

# Ram Island Light

**Boothbay, Maine**

## Directions

Ram Island is not accessible by car; the best way to see the light is by boat. Charters are available out of Boothbay Harbor. The lighthouse is not open to the public, though the grounds are open by appointment.

Latitude: 43° 48' 12" N
Longitude: 69° 36' 00" W

**Contact Information:**
**Ram Island Preservation**
**Society**
**Box 123**
**Boothbay, ME 04537**
**(207) 633-4727**

# Rockland Breakwater Light

First established in 1827 as a lantern at the end of Jameson Point at the entrance to Rockland Harbor, the permanent station on the Rockland Breakwater wasn't built until 1902. For many years, the light station was located at various points on the granite breakwater, which was built in the 1880s to protect the open harbor from nor'easters that caused problems for shipping vessels and waterfront buildings.

In 1888 a light at the end of the breakwater was built by order of President Cleveland, but it did not include a keeper's quarters and was not considered permanent. Charles Ames was named as keeper during this time. He was paid $25 per month to travel to the breakwater twice daily: at dusk to light the lamps and in the morning to extinguish the lamps. On foggy evenings, Ames would use a metal triangle to warn mariners of the approaching shore.

That light was replaced when President Harrison authorized the building of the current lighthouse, which is made of stone and brick and includes gambrel-style keeper's quarters. Originally equipped with a fourth-order Fresnel lens, the tower is 25 feet high and the 250-mm optic flashes white every 5 seconds, with a focal plane of 39 feet, for a range of 17 miles. The foghorn building is built into the main structure.

# Rockland Breakwater Light

### Rockland, Maine

Automated in 1964, the property is officially owned by the City of Rockland, but is leased by the American Lighthouse Foundation's Friends of the Rockland Breakwater chapter. Restorations made to the beacon include repainting the exterior and clearing the interior of hazardous waste. A float and ramp were also added to the site to eliminate the need to walk over the breakwater.

Rockland Breakwater Light is an active aid to navigation. It is open to the public on weekends from May to October.

## Directions

From Route 1 in Rockland, turn east on Waldo Avenue. Turn right on Samoset and follow it to the end, where there is a footpath to the lighthouse.

Latitude: 44° 06' 12" N
Longitude: 69° 04' 42" W

**Contact Information:**
**Friends of the Rockland Breakwater Lighthouse**
**P.O. Box 741**
**Rockland, ME 04841**
**www.rocklandlighthouse.com**

# Rockland Harbor Southwest Light

Marking Seal Ledge in Rockland Harbor, Rockland Harbor Southwest Light was built in the 1980s as a private aid to navigation. It was later approved by the Coast Guard.

The 44-foot tower was originally equipped with an electric marine lens. It now has a fifth-order Fresnel lens that flashes yellow every 2.5 seconds. Maine's newest lighthouse, the property is a private residence.

# Rockland Harbor Southwest Light

## Rockland, Maine

### Directions

From downtown Rockland, go south on Highway 73 for 1.9 miles to North Shore Drive. Turn left on North Shore Drive, drive for 0.9 mile, and turn left on a dirt road that leads to the light. The lighthouse is privately owned. Please respect the privacy of the owners.

Latitude: 44° 06' 26" N (approx.)
Longitude: 69° 06' 28" W (approx.)

**Contact Information:**
**City of Rockland**
**270 Pleasant Street**
**Rockland, ME 04841**
**(207) 594-8431**
**www.ci.rockland.me.us**

# Saddleback Ledge Light

Located on the 25-foot rocky point called Saddleback Ledge at the entrance to Isle au Haut Bay (part of East Penobscot Bay), Saddleback Ledge Light was established in 1839. Isle au Haut Bay is large; as a result, Saddleback's location at the entrance is essentially an isolated, distant outpost, vulnerable to weather and lonely for keepers.

Keepers were required to travel by boat out to the station, and, because of the height of the ledge walls, a derrick was installed in 1885 to transport people onto shore. This contraption consisted of a boom and tackle with a bosun's chair at the end that was swung out over the water. Unfortunately, the derrick was unsteady in the often-blustery winds and getting into the chair from a rocking boat was often a challenge; the derrick was consequently thought by many to be almost as dangerous as climbing out of the water.

Though subjected to severe winter storms for years, the original lighthouse still stands. With a granite tower of 42 feet, Saddleback Ledge Light was originally equipped with a fifth-order Fresnel lens, but has since been fitted with a 300-mm optic. The light shines at 54 feet above sea level for a range of 9 miles, flashing white every 6 seconds. There were brick keeper's

118

# Saddleback Ledge Light

## Vinalhaven, Maine

quarters attached to the tower, but they were demolished in a Green Beret assault exercise in 1960, and there are no other buildings on the ledge. The station was automated in 1954.

### Directions

Saddleback Ledge Light is best seen by boat. Charters are available out of Rockland, Vinalhaven, or Stonington. The station is not open to the public.

Latitude: 44° 00' 54" N
Longitude: 68° 43' 36" W

**Contact Information:**
**U.S. Coast Guard**
**Aides to Navigation Team**
**P.O. Box 5000**
**Southwest Harbor, ME 04679**
**www.uscg.mil**

# Seguin Island Light

One of the highest lighthouses in Maine, Seguin Island Light sits atop Seguin Island, 2 miles from the mouth of the Kennebec River.

The first tower was built in 1795 by order of George Washington. Its single lantern was reflected entirely toward the ocean. Count John Polersky became the beacon's first keeper as a reward for his Revolutionary War service. Polersky complained about the low salary, stating that "The first three years will cost me money out of my own pocket." However, the government was not sympathetic, and it is said that Polersky died miserable after storms had destroyed his home, gardens, and boats.

Damaged by a storm, the original tower was replaced in 1820 with a stone tower holding the original lamp. In 1842, additional lanterns were installed, increasing the light's range to a reported 20 miles. Unfortunately, the second tower did not weather the elements well, and was deemed unsafe and inadequate for needed optic upgrades by mid-century.

# Seguin Island Light

## Seguin Island, Maine

In 1857, the existing 53-foot granite block tower was built. Still operating with the first-order Fresnel lens installed then (the only such lens in Maine), Seguin Island Light shines a continuous white light at 180 feet above sea level and has a range of 18 miles.

The Friends of Seguin Island, an all-volunteer nonprofit group consisting mostly of local residents, won possession of the beacon in 1989. Since then, they have performed many major repairs, including replacing the tower's roof.

A small museum and gift shop are presently housed in the keeper's quarters, and a volunteer caretaker is assigned to the living quarters each summer. A 1,100-foot tramway nicknamed the "Seguin Express" that carried passengers and cargo up the steep quarter-mile climb from boathouse to lighthouse remains on the property. Passengers were banned from riding the tramway in the mid-20th century when a cable broke and a woman was badly hurt.

Located in a historic bird sanctuary, the light is an active aid to navigation.

## Directions

Seguin Island is not accessible by car; the lighthouse is best viewed by boat. Private charters are available out of Bath and Boothbay Harbor.

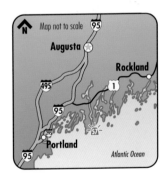

Latitude: 43° 42' 30" N
Longitude: 69° 45' 30" W

**Contact Information:**
Friends of Seguin Island, Inc.
Box 866
Bath, ME 04530
(207) 443-4808
www.seguinisland.org

# Spring Point Ledge Light

Requested for several years by shipping lines to mark the dangerous Spring Point Ledge for passenger vessels, Spring Point Ledge Light was finally authorized by Congress in 1895. Stalled due to bureaucratic problems and inclement weather, the tower was finally lit by keeper William A. Lane on May 24, 1897. Spring Point Ledge Light is located on the west side of the entrance to Portland Harbor. It is one of three remaining sparkplug-style stations in Maine.

Built on an iron caisson, the foundation was vulnerable to heavy seas and ice floes; to strengthen the base, in 1951 the government built a granite foundation around it. With a tower height of 54 feet above sea level, the brick tower was originally equipped with a fifth-order Fresnel lens. It now has a 300-mm optic that flashes white every 6 seconds for a range of 14 miles. The station has an electric foghorn and the keeper's quarters are contained

# Spring Point Ledge Light

## South Portland, Maine

within the tower. Automated in 1934, Spring Point Ledge Light is an active aid to navigation.

Unlike other sparkplug-style lighthouses, Spring Point Ledge Light is accessible to pedestrians. The Army Corps of Engineers constructed a breakwater leading out to the lighthouse in 1950.

The Spring Point Ledge Light Trust, a chapter of the Portland Harbor Museum, gained ownership of the lighthouse in 1998 through the Maine Lights program. The group often hosts open houses at the lighthouse in summer in order to educate the public about Spring Point Ledge Light and lighthouses in general.

## Directions

From I-95 (Maine Turnpike) take exit 7 and continue straight out of the tollbooth, ignoring other exits for about 2 miles until the road ends at Route 1 (traffic light). Turn left onto Route 1 (Main Street) and bear east at the fourth traffic light onto Broadway. Stay on Broadway until it ends (stop sign) at Pickett Road and turn left on Pickett. Go to Fort Road and turn left. Follow Fort Road through the Southern Maine Technical College campus until it ends at the water. Portland Harbor Museum is on your right.

Latitude: 43° 39' 06" N
Longitude: 70° 13' 24" W

Contact Information:
Spring Point Ledge Light Trust
P.O. Box 2311
South Portland, ME 04106
(207) 767-7488
www.springpointlight.org

# Squirrel Point Light

One of four lighthouses in Arrowsic, Squirrel Point Light is located on Arrowsic Island in the Kennebec River. Built in 1898 to support the shipping industry on the Kennebec, the facility is similar in design to that of Doubling Point Light, also located in Arrowsic.

The 25-foot tower is constructed of wood on a stone block foundation. Originally equipped with a fifth-order Fresnel lens, Squirrel Point Light now has a 250-mm optic that shines at 33 feet above sea level for a range of 9 miles. The light flashes red for 3 seconds on, 3 seconds off.

The original Victorian wood-frame keeper's quarters still stand and have recently been renovated by a private owner. The foghorn building built in 1902 is attached to the tower. There are also an oil house, boathouse, garage, and barn.

# Squirrel Point Light

## Arrowsic, Maine

### Directions

From Highway 1, east of Bath, take Route 127 south to Bald Head Road. Turn right onto Bald Head Road and follow until it ends—about a mile. From there, a footpath leads south for about a mile to the lighthouse. The lighthouse is not open to the public.

Latitude: 43° 49' 00" N
Longitude: 69° 48' 06" W

**Contact Information:**
**Squirrel Point Associates, Inc.**
**P.O. Box 1098**
**Portland, Maine 04104**

# Tenants Harbor Light

Built in 1857 to support the once-busy shipping industry at St. George, Tenants Harbor Light is located on Southern Island to mark Tenants Harbor for mariners traveling along Two Bush Channel.

Built of stone on a brick foundation, the 27-foot tower was equipped with a fourth-order Fresnel lens. The wood fog bell building still stands, as do the Cape Cod–style keeper's quarters. An oil house, storage building, and covered passageway are also extant.

Tenants Harbor Light was deactivated in 1933. The property was put up for auction in the 1970s and purchased by artist Andrew Wyeth. His son, artist Jamie Wyeth, now owns the estate and has converted the bell tower into a studio. Several of the younger Wyeth's paintings have featured or been inspired by Tenants Harbor Light and Southern Island.

# Tenants Harbor Light

## St. George, Maine

### Directions

Tenants Harbor Light is privately owned and not accessible by car. Boat charters are available out of Owls Head to see the lighthouse by water.

Latitude: 43° 57' 40" N
Longitude: 69° 11' 05" W

**Contact information:
Privately owned.**

# Two Bush Island Light

Two Bush Island Light was allegedly named by fishermen who used two pine trees on the island as daymarkers to help guide them through Two Bush Channel. A more effective beacon was built in 1897. The 42-foot tower was originally equipped with a fifth-order Fresnel lens, but now operates with a VRB-25 optic that flashes white every 5 seconds.

Shining at 65 feet above sea level, Two Bush Island Light has a range of 17 miles. The keeper's quarters were demolished in 1970, but the brick fog-horn building still stands. Automated in 1964, the station is an active aid to navigation owned by the U.S. Fish and Wildlife Service.

One rather romantic anecdote from the turn of the 20th century relates that the keeper's dog awoke him one night just in time to save the two-man crew of the schooner *Clara Bella*'s dory, which had overturned. One of the rescued men wanted to adopt the dog, but the keeper would not consider it.

# Two Bush Island Light

## Spruce Head, Maine

### Directions

Two Bush Island Light is best seen by boat. Charters are available out of Tenants Harbor in St. George or Owls Head. Please keep in mind that because the light is located on a wildlife refuge, it is necessary to be sensitive to the needs of nesting seabirds; going ashore is not permitted from April 1 to August 31. The lighthouse is not open to the public.

Latitude: 43° 57' 51" N
Longitude: 69° 04' 26" W

**Contact Information:**
**U.S. Fish and Wildlife Service**
**Petit Manan National Wildlife Refuge**
**P.O. Box 279**
**Milbridge, ME 04658**
**(207) 546-2124**
**http://petitmanan.fws.gov/**

# West Quoddy Head Light

Established in 1808 by order of President Jefferson, West Quoddy Head Light marks the west entrance to Quoddy Roads in the Bay of Fundy.

In an area prone to heavy fog such as this one, it was important to protect mariners with some kind of audible signal. A fog signal was implemented in 1820, but it consisted of a hand-struck bell manned by the keeper. Over the years, four other bells were tried—weighing as much as 1,500 pounds—but it was a chore to sound the alarm. Attempts were made to automate the ringing, but they proved to be ineffective. The issue was resolved in 1869 when a Daboll fog whistle was installed.

West Quoddy Head Light was rebuilt in 1858 by order of President Buchanan and its distinctive red-and-white-striped color scheme was added shortly thereafter. Despite its name, West Quoddy Head Light is the easternmost lighthouse in the United States and offers a stunning view of both the coast of Maine and of New Brunswick, Canada. The brick tower is 49 feet tall and the third-order Fresnel lens installed in 1858 still operates, shining at 83 feet above sea level for a range of 18 miles.

# West Quoddy Head Light

## Lubec, Maine

The Victorian keeper's quarters, built in 1858, still stand and are home to a small seasonal museum and visitor center. The 1887 brick foghorn building also remains. Automated in 1988, the light is an active aid to navigation, with two white flashes every 15 seconds. The station, located in Quoddy Head State Park, is open to the public.

### Directions

From Highway 1 in Whiting, go east on Highway 189. Turn south on Lubec Road. Turn east on Quoddy Head Road, go all the way into Quoddy Head State Park, and follow signs to the lighthouse.

Latitude: 44° 48' 54" N
Longitude: 66° 57' 00" W

**Contact Information:**
**West Quoddy Head Light**
**Keepers' Association**
**P.O. Box 378**
**Lubec, ME 04652**
**(207) 733-2180**
**www.westquoddy.com**

# Whaleback Light

One of the southernmost lighthouses in Maine, Whaleback Light marks the entrance to the Piscataqua River at Portsmouth (New Hampshire) Harbor.

First established in 1820, a permanent station with a 48-foot tower was built in 1831 by order of President Jackson. The tower quickly fell into disrepair, however, so it was refurbished in the mid-19th century. When that tower, too, became worn, it was dismantled. However, part of the tower was used as a fog bell building for the subsequent station. Unfortunately, the fog signal building is now gone.

Built in 1872, the current lighthouse is 50 feet tall and shines at 59 feet above sea level for a range of 18 miles. Made of granite blocks on a stone foundation, the tower contains keeper's quarters. The 1855 fourth-order Fresnel lens that was saved from the second tower was replaced with a DCB-224 optic in 1963 when the station was automated. That optic was in turn replaced by a rotating VRB-25 aerobeacon that flashes white twice every 10 seconds.

An active aid to navigation, the lighthouse is not open to the public.

# Whaleback Light

## Kittery, Maine

### Directions

From I-95 in Kittery, take exit 2, Route 236. Go left off the ramp on 236. Follow halfway around a traffic circle and continue on Route 236. Go through downtown Kittery and Route 236 will become Route 103. Continue on Route 103 across the Kittery Point Bridge and through Fort McClary. Continue to Chauncey Creek Road and bear right. Take the first right on Gerrish Island Lane, go across a small bridge, and turn right on Pocahontas Road. You'll be in a residential area, but do not be alarmed. Go to the end of Pocahontas Road to Fort Foster, and into the park to the end, where you will be able to see the lighthouse.

Latitude: 43° 03' 30" N
Longitude: 70° 41' 48" W

**Contact Information:**
**U.S. Coast Guard**
**Aides to Navigation Team**
**P.O. Box 5000**
**Southwest Harbor, ME 04679**
**www.uscg.mil**

# Whitehead Light

Marking the Muscle Ridge Channel at the southern entrance to Penobscot Bay, Whitehead Light was built of stone in 1807 by order of President Jefferson. Shortly after its establishment, Whitehead Light became entrenched in scandal. After an unusually large number of requests for more whale oil from the station's first keeper, investigators from the Lighthouse Board discovered that the keeper was selling the oil to local merchants for a hefty profit. He was immediately dismissed.

A second station, made of granite, was built at the site in 1830, but was torn down when, in 1852, a third structure was built by order of President Fillmore. This is the lighthouse we see today.

Serving the granite industry and related shipping activities, the granite tower stands 41 feet high. Its 1855 third-order Fresnel lens was replaced in 1982 with a 300-mm optic that shines at 75 feet above sea level with a green light occulting every 4 seconds; it can be seen for 6 miles. The 1891 wood-frame keeper's quarters still stand and are under renovation to be used as a museum and for educational purposes. The brick fog signal building, built in 1888, is also on the property. There are also an

## St. George, Maine

oil house, garage, boathouse, schoolhouse, wharf, and the foundations of several buildings that no longer stand.

Owned by Pine Island Camp, the property is the location of a summer camp program and is not open to the public. The camp has established a three-week Whitehead Lightkeepers Program for teenage boys and girls who are interested in learning how to restore and preserve a lighthouse. Among other activities, campers learn about the history of the light station and take part in logging each day's activities.

### Directions

Whitehead Island is not accessible by car; the lighthouse can be seen by boat. Private charters are available out of Owls Head and Port Clyde.

Latitude: 43° 58' 42" N
Longitude: 69° 07' 30" W

**Contact Information:**
Pine Island Camp/
Whitehead Lightkeepers
P.O. Box 242
Brunswick, ME 04011
(207) 729-7714
www.pineisland.org

# Whitlocks Mill Light

First established as a tree lantern in 1892, a permanent station called Whitlocks Mill Light was built in 1909 to mark the south bank of the St. Croix River. The station is so named for the mill operator whom the Coast Guard hired to maintain the original tree lantern. It is the westernmost light on the St. Croix and the northernmost station in the United States. Whitlocks Mill Light was built largely to support the shipping traffic that traveled the river into Calais. The area is very picturesque, particularly the high, rocky riverbanks below Calais and out toward the ocean.

# Whitlocks Mill Light

## Calais, Maine

Constructed of a unique brick with a ceramic tile lining (a material used in only one other Maine lighthouse, Rockland Breakwater Light), the 25-foot tower sits on a granite and timber foundation, giving it a total height of 32 feet above sea level. Originally equipped with a fourth-order Fresnel lens, the tower now has a 250-mm lens that was installed in 1969 when the station was automated. The light flashes green 3 seconds on and 3 seconds off and has a range of 5 miles.

The 1909 Dutch colonial keeper's quarters still stand and are used as a private dwelling. The fog bell building constructed in 1910 still exists, as do an oil house and storage building.

## Directions

Whitlocks Mill Light is privately owned and is not open to the public. It can be seen by boat from the St. Croix River.

Latitude: 45° 09' 48" N
Longitude: 67° 13' 36" W

**Contact Information:**
**St. Croix Historical Society**
**P.O. Box 242**
**Calais, ME 04619**
**(207) 454-2604**

# Winter Harbor Light

Built in 1856 by order of President Pierce to mark Winter Harbor for shipping vessels, Winter Harbor Light is located on Mark Island west of the Schoodic Peninsula.

In its day, the 19-foot brick lighthouse stood at a full height of 37 feet above sea level and was equipped with a fifth-order Fresnel lens. Replaced by a bell buoy in 1933 because of the decline in commercial marine travel in the area, the station was deactivated and sold into private ownership. The two-story Victorian keeper's quarters are a private residence.

# Winter Harbor Light

### Also known as Mark Island Light
### Winter Harbor, Maine

### Directions

Because Mark Island is not accessible by car, and because the property is privately owned and therefore not open to the public, Winter Harbor Light is best seen from a boat. Charters are available from Bar Harbor and Winter Harbor.

Latitude: 44° 21' 41" N
Longitude: 68° 05' 16" W

**Contact Information:**
**Privately owned.**

# Wood Island Light

Marking the south entrance to Wood Island Harbor and the entrance to the Saco River, Wood Island Light is located on the east side of the island. The island itself is said to be home to the ghost of a lobsterman who was mortally wounded by an intoxicated young drifter inhabiting the island. After shooting the lobsterman, the young man panicked and committed suicide.

The first tower on Wood Island was built of granite blocks in 1808 by order of President Jefferson. In 1858, to update the station's usefulness, the current station was built under President Buchanan. It, too, is built of granite, and was originally equipped with a fourth-order Fresnel lens. In 1972, a VRB-25 optic was installed and the lantern was removed from the tower. After receiving several complaints about the unattractive "headless" tower, a new lantern room was added to Wood Island Light. Today, the 47-foot tower standing at 71 feet above sea level can be seen for 18 miles with an alternating white and green flash every 5 seconds.

The fog bell tower has been removed, but the bell is on display at Vine's Landing in Biddeford. The two-story Dutch colonial keeper's quarters still stand, as do an oil house, storage building, and wooden walkway. The

# Wood Island Light

## Biddeford, Maine

buildings are leased to the Wood Island Lighthouse Society, a chapter of the American Lighthouse Foundation, and the island is owned by the Maine Audubon Society. The Wood Island Lighthouse Society recently began offering tours of the tower and keeper's dwelling.

## Directions

Wood Island is not accessible by car, and Wood Island Light is not open to the public except through tours arranged with the Friends of Wood Island Lighthouse, so the lighthouse is best seen by boat. Private charters are available out of Biddeford, Kennebunkport, or South Portland.

Latitude: 43° 27' 24" N
Longitude: 70° 19' 42" W

Contact Information:
Friends of Wood Island Lighthouse
P.O. Box 26
Biddeford Pool, ME 04006
www.woodislandlighthouse.org

# Appendix

## Maine Calendar of Events

**January**
Bath Antique Show and Sale, Bath (207-443-8983)
New Year's Out Right Ride, Woolwich (207-633-5065)
Oxford Hills Snowfest, Norway (207-743-6483)
Snodeo, Rangeley (207-864-7336,
    www.rangeleysnowmobile.com/snodeo.htm)

**February**
Katahdin Winterfest, Millinocket (207-723-4443,
    www.katahdinmaine.com)
Moosestompers, Houlton (207-532-4216)
Mushers Bowl–Winter Carnival, Bridgton (207-647-3472,
    www.mushersbowl.com)

**March**
Bangor Boat Show, Bangor (207-947-5555)
Can-Am Crown International Sled Dog Races, Fort Kent
    (www.can-am.sjv.net/main.htm)
Maine Handicapped Ski-A-Thon, Bethel (800-639-7770,
    www.skimhs.org)
Maine Maple Sunday, fourth Sunday in March, various locations
    (207-287-3491, www.getrealmaine.com/
    visit/maine_maple_sunday.html)
Mars Hills Winterfest, Mars Hill (207-864-5364)

**April**
Bangor Garden Show, Bangor (207-596-0376,
    www.bangorgardenshow.com)
Bust 'n Burn and Parrothead Festival, Sunday River
    (207-824-3000)
Fishermen's Festival, Boothbay Harbor (800-266-8422,
    www.boothbayharbor.com/events_fishermensfest.asp)
Portland Home Show, Portland (800-237-6024,
    www.homeshows.com)

**May**
Appalachian Extreme Adventure Race, Sunday River Ski Resort,
    Bethel (207-836-2772)
Arcady Music Festival, Bar Harbor (207-288-2141,
    www.arcady.org)
Down East Spring Birding Festival, Whiting (207-733-2201,
    www.downeastbirdfest.org)
Family Fun Festival, Biddeford (207-946-7079)
MooseMainea, Greenville (888-876-2778,
    www.mooseheadlake.org)

| | |
|---|---|
| **June** | Acadian Festival, Madawaska (207-728-4696, www.townofmadawaska.com/cc.html) |
| | Annual Chamber Music Festival, Ogunquit (207-646-6170) |
| | Bar Harbor Chamber of Commerce Art Show, Bar Harbor (207-288-5103) |
| | Beachfest and other summerlong activities, Old Orchard Beach (www.oldorchardbeachmaine.com/Activity.htm) |
| | Friendship Sloop Days, Rockland (207-832-6828) |
| | Jazz and Blues Showcase, Kingfield (207-265-4037) |
| | Kingfield Flowerfest, Kingfield (207-265-4037) |
| | La Kermesse Franco-American Festival, Biddeford (www.biddefordmaine.org/) |
| | Lupine Festival, Deer Isle (207-367-2420) |
| | South Berwick Strawberry Festival, South Berwick (207-384-3208, www.southberwickstrawberryfestival.com) |
| | Summer Solstice Night, Rockland (207-596-0376) |
| | The Whatever Family Festival, Augusta (www.augustamaine.com/whatever_calendar.html) |
| | Windjammer Days, Boothbay Harbor (www.boothbayharbor.com/events_windjammer.asp) |
| **July** | '50s and '60s Car Meet and Antique Aeroplane Show, Owls Head (207-594-4418, www.ohtm.org) |
| | Annual House and Garden Tour, Camden (207-236-7468) |
| | Bowdoin International Music Festival, Brunswick (207-373-1400, www.bowdoinfestival.org) |
| | Greek Heritage Festival, Saco (207-284-5651) |
| | HarborFest, Wells (207-646-2451) |
| | L.L. Bean Summer Concert Series, Freeport (800-559-0747, ext. 37222) |
| | Maine International Film Festival, Waterville (207-861-8138, www.miff.org) |
| | Maine Potato Blossom Festival, Fort Fairfield (www.potatoblossom.org) |
| | Maine Shakespeare Festival, Bangor (207-942-3333, www.ptc.maineguide.com) |
| | North Atlantic Blues Festival, Rockland (207-593-1189) |
| | Old Orchard Parade and Sandcastle Contest, Old Orchard Beach (207-934-2500) |
| | Saltwater Music Festival, Brunswick (888-757-SALT, www.saltfest.com) |
| | Yarmouth Clam Festival, Yarmouth (207-846-3984, www.clamfestival.com) |
| **August** | Academy Antiques Show, Blue Hill (207-374-5026) |
| | Arts and Artisans Fair, Lovell (207-925-1135) |
| | Blueberry Festival, Rangeley (207-864-5364) |
| | Festival de Joie, Lewiston (207-782-6231, www.festivaldejoie.org) |

| | |
|---|---|
| **August** *cont.* | Great Falls Balloon Festival, Lewiston/Auburn (800-639-6331, www.greatfallsballoonfestival.org) |
| | Heritage Days, Carthage (207-562-7090) |
| | International Festival, Calais (http://visitcalais.com/festival) |
| | Maine Lobster Festival, Harbor Park, Rockland (207-596-0367, www.mainelobsterfestival.com) |
| | Maine Wild Blueberry Festival and Union Fair, Union (207-785-3281 [summer] or 207-236-8009 [off-season], www.union-fair.com) |
| | Naples Classic Boat Show, Naples (207-693-6226) |
| | National Folk Festival, Bangor (207-992-2630, www.nationalfolkfestival.com) |
| | Northeast Silent Film Festival, Bucksport (207-469-0924) |
| | Passamaquoddy Indian Days Celebration, Pleasant Point Reservation, Perry (207-853-2600, www.eastport.net/events) |
| | Sidewalk Art Festival, Portland (800-464-1213) |
| | Skowhegan State Fair, Skowhegan (207-474-2947, www.skowheganstatefair.com) |
| | Transportation Festival and Aerobatic Spectacular, Owls Head (207-594-4418, www.ohtm.org) |
| | Wild Blueberry Festival, Machias (www.machiasblueberry.com) |
| | |
| **September** | Bluegrass Festival, Brunswick (877-872-4321, www.thomaspointbeach.com/bluegrass.info.shtml) |
| | Capriccio Festival of Kites, Ogunquit (207-646-6170) |
| | Car Show and Parade, Old Orchard Beach (207-934-2500, www.oldorchardbeachmaine.com) |
| | Cascade Park Celebration, Bangor (207-947-1018) |
| | Fall Foliage 5K Run and Great Western Chili Cookoff, Waterford (207-583-2603) |
| | Festival Days, Eliot (207-439-5033) |
| | Fiddler's Contest and Country Music Show, Kennebunkport (207-967-0857) |
| | International Seaplane Fly-In Weekend, Greenville (www.mooseheadlake.org) |
| | Septemberfest, Kittery (888-587-6246) |
| | Wells Chili Fest, Wells (207-646-2451) |
| | |
| **October** | Bath Autumn Fest, Bath (207-442-7291) |
| | Camden Fall Festival, Camden (207-236-4404) |
| | Fall Arts and Crafts Fair, Caribou (800-722-6372) |
| | Fall Fling, Searsport (207-548-6742) |
| | Fall Foliage Festival, Boothbay (207-633-4727, www.boothbayharbor.com) |
| | Fall Frolic, Ogunquit (207-646-2939) |
| | Festival of Scarecrows, Rockland (207-596-6457) |
| | Fiddlehead Fine Art Show and Silent Auction, Houlton (207-532-2900) |
| | Fryeburg Fair, Fryeburg (207-935-3268, www.fryeburgfair.com) |

| October *cont.* | Ghost Train, Boothbay (207-633-4727, www.boothbayharbor.com) |
|---|---|
| | Halloween in the Valley, Mexico (207-364-2051) |
| | Harvestfest, York (207-363-4422) |
| | Medley of Colors Quilt Show, Windham (207-637-2675) |
| | Oktoberfest, Rumford (207-364-4561) |
| | Presque Isle Fall Arts and Crafts Fair, Presque Isle (207-764-0491) |
| | Pumpkin Patch Weekend, Kennebunkport (207-985-9723) |
| | Punkin Fiddle Contest, Wells (http://punkinfiddle.org) |
| | Waterville Jazz Festival, Waterville (207-680-2055) |
| | |
| November | An Old Fashioned Christmas, Bath (207-443-7291) |
| | Christmas Craft Show, Augusta (207-946-7079) |
| | Dickens of a Christmas, Fort Kent (800-233-3563) |
| | Festival of Lights, Rockland (207-596-0376) |
| | Holiday Craft Market, Rockport (207-596-0376) |
| | Lighting of the Nubble, York Beach (207-363-1040) |
| | St. Patrick's Holiday Fair, Brewer (207-862-5380) |
| | Tree Lighting Ceremony and Santa Parade, Caribou (800-722-7648) |
| | United Maine Craftsmen Thanksgiving Craft Show, Brewer (207-621-2818, www.unitedmainecraftsmen.com) |
| | |
| December | Christmas at Norlands Living History Center, Livermore (207-897-4366, www.norlands.org) |
| | Christmas Prelude, Kennebunkport (www.christmasprelude.com) |
| | Festival of Lights Parade, Bangor (207-945-4400) |
| | Festival of Trees, Farmington (207-778-4215) |
| | Harbor Lights Festival, Boothbay Harbor (207-633-2353, www.boothbayharbor.com) |
| | Holiday Arts Fair, Bar Harbor (207-288-5008) |
| | Holiday Stroll, Skowhegan (207-474-3621) |
| | New Years Portland, Portland (www.newyearsportland.com) |

## Accommodations and Other Sites of Interest in Maine

**Arrowsic/Bath/Boothbay/Brunswick/Georgetown/Phippsburg/Southport**
*Other Sites of Interest:*
Eagle Island, Harpswell (207-624-6080)
Hamilton Sanctuary, West Bath (207-781-2330)
Historic Topsham Walking Tour, Topsham (207-725-1718)
Maine Maritime Museum, Bath (207-443-1316, www.bathmaine.com)
Old Stone Schoolhouse Museum, Georgetown (207-371-9065)
Woolwich Historical Society Rural Farmhouse & Barn Museum, Woolwich
 (207-443-4833)

*Accommodations:*
Atrium Inn and Convention Center, Brunswick (207-729-5555)
Bailey Island Motel, Bailey Island (207-833-2886, www.baileyislandmotel.com)
Black Lantern Bed and Breakfast, Topsham (888-306-4165,
    www.blacklanternbandb.com)
Brunswick Bed and Breakfast, Brunswick (800-299-4914,
    www.brunswickbandb.com)
Captain's Watch Bed and Breakfast, Harpswell (207-725-0979)
Cod Cove Inn, Edgecomb (800-882-9586, www.codcoveinn.com)
Coveside Bed & Breakfast, Georgetown (800-232-5490, www.covesidebandb.com)
Driftwood Inn, Bailey Island (207-833-5461)
Fairhaven Inn, Bath (888-443-4391)
Galen C. Moses House, Bath (888-442-8771, www.galenmoses.com)
Grey Havens Inn, Georgetown (800-431-2316, www.greyhavens.com)
Hodgdon Island Inn, Boothbay (207-633-7474, www.hodgdonislandinn.com)
Holland House Cottage B & B, Brunswick (207-729-0709,
    www.hollandhousecottage.com)
The Inn at Bath, Bath (800-423-0964, www.innatbath.com)
The Kennebec Inn, Bath (888-595-1664)
Little Island Motel, Orr's Island (207-833-2392, www.littleislandmotel.com)
Middle Bay Farm Bed & Breakfast, Brunswick (207-373-1375,
    www.middlebayfarm.com)
The Mooring B&B, Georgetown (207-371-2790)
Parkwood Inn, Brunswick (800-349-7181, www.parkwoodinn.com)
Popham Beach Bed & Breakfast, Phippsburg (207-389-2409,
    www.pophambeachbandb.com)
Pryor House Bed and Breakfast, Bath (207-443-1146)

**Bar Harbor/Bass Harbor/Cranberry Isles/Frenchboro**
*Other Sites of Interest:*
Abbe Museum, Bar Harbor (207-288-3519, www.abbemuseum.org)
Acadia National Park, Mount Desert Island (207-288-3338, www.nps.gov/acad/)
Oceanarium & Lobster Hatchery, Bar Harbor (207-288-5005,
    www.theoceanarium.com)

*Accommodations:*
1898 Yankee Lady Inn, Bar Harbor (800-971-4999, www.yankeeladyinn.com)
Acacia House Hotel, Bar Harbor (800-551-5399, www.acaciabarharbor.com)
Acadia Hotel, Bar Harbor (207-288-5721, www.acadiahotel.com)
Anne's White Columns Inn, Bar Harbor (800-321-6379,
    www.anneswhitecolumns.com)
Atlantean, Bar Harbor (800-722-6671, www.atlanteaninn.com)
Atlantic Oakes, Bar Harbor (800-336-2463, www.barharbor.com)
Bar Harbor Manor, Bar Harbor (207-288-3829, www.barharbormanor.com)
Bass Cottage Inn, Bar Harbor (207-288-1234, www.basscottage.com)
Bayview Inn, Bar Harbor (800-356-3585, www.bahabamaine.com)
The Birches, Southwest Harbor (207-244-5182)
Black Friar Inn, Bar Harbor (207-288-5091, www.blackfriarinn.com)

Captain Bennett House, Southwest Harbor (207-244-9627,
    www.captainbennett.com)
Castlemaine Inn 1886, Bar Harbor (800-338-4563, www.castlemaineinn.com)
The Claremont Hotel, Southwest Harbor (800-244-5036,
    www.acadia.net/claremont)
Coach Stop Inn, Bar Harbor (207-288-9886, www.coachstopinn.com)
Graycote Inn, Bar Harbor (207-288-3044, www.graycoteinn.com)
Harbor View Motel & Cottages, Southwest Harbor (800-538-6463)
Holbrook House, Bar Harbor (207-288-4970, www.holbrookhouse.com)
Holland Inn, Bar Harbor (207-288-4804)
The Island House, Southwest Harbor (207-244-5180)
The Kedge Bed and Breakfast, Bar Harbor (800-597-8306, www.thekedge.com)
The Kingsleigh Inn, Southwest Harbor (207-244-5302, www.kingsleighinn.com)
Ledgelawn Inn, Bar Harbor (800-274-5334)
Manor House Inn, Bar Harbor (800-437-0088, www.barharbormanorhouse.com)
Mansell House, Southwest Harbor (207-244-5625)
The Maples Inn, Bar Harbor (207-288-3443, www.maplesinn.com)
Mira Monte Inn & Suites, Bar Harbor (800-553-5109, www.miramonte.com)
Quimby House Inn, Bar Harbor (207-288-5811, www.quimbyhouse.com)
Seacroft Inn, Bar Harbor (800-824-9694, www.seacroftinn.com)
Stonethrow Cottage, Bar Harbor (800-769-3668, www.stonethrowcottage.com)
Ullikana Bed & Breakfast, Bar Harbor, (207-288-9552, www.ullikana.com)

## Biddeford
*Other Sites of Interest:*
East Point Audubon Sanctuary, Biddeford (207-781-2330)
Saco Heath, Saco (www.sacobaytrails.org/heath.shtml)
Saco Museum, Saco (207-283-3861, www.sacomuseum.org)
Scarborough Marsh and Nature Center, Scarborough (207-883-5100)
Wells National Estuarine Reserve, Wells (207-646-1555, www.wellsreserve.org)

*Accommodations:*
Bay View Cottages & Neptune Motel, Saco (207-282-2637)
Biddeford Motel, Biddeford (207-284-8924, www.biddefordmotel.com)
Billow House, Ocean Park (888-767-7776, www.billowhouse.com)
Crown 'N' Anchor Inn, Saco (207-282-3829)
Dallaire's Motel & Cottages, Biddeford (207-284-4100)
Eastview Motel, Saco (207-282-2362)
Hobson House Celtic Inn, Saco (207-284-4113, www.hobsonhouse.com)
Millbrook Motel, Scarborough (800-371-6005, www.millbrookmotel.com)
Nautilus by the Sea, Ocean Park (800-981-7018, www.nautilusbythesea.com)
Saco Motel, Saco (207-284-6952)
Sleepy Hollow Motel, Biddeford (207-282-0031)
Sunrise Motel, Saco (207-283-3883)
Wagon Wheel Motel, Saco (207-284-6387)

## Blue Hill Bay/East Blue Hill
*Other Sites of Interest:*
Holbrook Island Sanctuary, Brooksville (207-326-4012)

**Blue Hill Bay/East Blue Hill** *cont.*
*Accommodations:*
The Blue Hill Inn, Blue Hill (207-374-2844, www.bluehillinn.com)
The Brooklin Inn, Brooklin (207-359-2777, www.brooklininn.com)
Captain Isaac Merrill Inn, Blue Hill (877-374-2555, www.captainmerrillinn.com)
Eggemoggin Reach B&B, Brooksville (888-625-8866)
First Light Bed & Breakfast, East Blue Hill (207-374-5879,
    www.firstlightbandb.com)
Goose Cove Lodge, Sunset (800-728-1963, www.goosecovelodge.com)
Heritage Motor Inn, Blue Hill (207-374-5646)
Inn at Blue Poppy, Sedgwick (866-332-6664, www.bluepoppygarden.com)
Oakland House Seaside Resort, Brooksville (800-359-7352,
    www.oaklandhouse.com)
The Orland House B&B, Orland (207-469-1144, www.orlandhousebb.com)
Surry Inn, Surry (800-742-3414, www.surreyinn.com)

**Calais**
*Other Sites of Interest:*
Moosehorn National Wildlife Refuge, Baring (207-454-7161, moosehorn.fws.gov)

*Accommodations:*
Calais Motor Inn, Calais (207-454-7111)
Downeaster Motel, South Calais (207-454-3376)
Home Sweet Home Bed and Breakfast, Alexander (207-454-3628)
International Motel, Calais (207-454-7515)
Redclyffe Shore Motel, Robbinston (207-454-3270)

**Camden/Islesboro/Monhegan Island/Rockport/Vinalhaven**
*Other Sites of Interest:*
Center for Maine Contemporary Art, Rockport (207-236-2875,
    www.artsmaine.org)
Merryspring Nature Park and Education Center, Camden (207-236-2239,
    www.merryspring.org)
State of Maine Cheese Co., Rockport (800-762-8895, www.cheese-me.com)

*Accommodations:*
Beloin's on the Maine Coast, Camden (207-236-3262, www.beloins.com)
Black Horse Inn, Camden (207-236-6800)
Blue Harbor House, Camden (207-236-3196, www.blueharborhouse.com)
Camden Harbour Inn, Camden (800-236-4266, www.camdenharbourinn.com)
Camden Riverhouse Hotel, Camden (800-755-7483, www.camdenmaine.com)
Cedar Crest Motel, Camden (207-236-4839, www.cedarcrestmotel.com)
Cedarholm Garden Bay Inn, Camden (207-236-3886, www.cedarholm.com)
Claddagh Motel & Suites, Rockport (207-594-8479, www.claddaghmotel.com)
Country Inn at Camden/Rockport, Camden (207-236-2725,
    www.countryinnmaine.com)
Dark Harbor House, Islesboro (207-734-6669,
    www.darkharborhouse.com)
Green Gables Inn, Camden (207-230-0088)

Hartstone Inn, Camden (800-788-4823, www.hartstoneinn.com)
High Tide Inn on the Ocean, Camden, (207-236-3724, www.hightideinn.com)
Island Inn, Monhegan Island, (207-596-0371, www.islandinnmonhegan.com)
Island View Inn, Rockport (207-596-0040)
The Lodge & Cottages at Camden Hills, Camden (207-236-8478,
     www.thelodgeatcamdenhills.com)
Lord Camden Inn, Camden (800-336-4325, www.lordcamdeninn.com)
Oakland Seashore Motel & Cottages, Rockport (207-594-8104)
Pilgrim's Inn, Deer Isle (888-778-7505, www.pilgrimsinn.com)
Samoset Resort, Camden (800-341-1650, www.samoset.com)
Schooner Bay Motor Inn, Rockport (207-236-2205)
Spruce Ridge Inn, Rockport (207-594-6689)
Strawberry Hill Seaside Inn, Rockport (207-594-5462)
Tidewater Motel, Vinalhaven (207-863-4618)
Towne Motel, Camden (207-236-3377)
Victorian by the Sea, Camden (800-382-9817, www.victorianbythesea.com)
White Gates Inn, Rockport (207-594-4625)
Whitehall Inn, Camden (207-236-3391)

## Cape Elizabeth/Portland/South Portland
*Other Sites of Interest:*
Crescent Beach State Park, Cape Elizabeth (207-799-5871)
Fort Williams Park, Cape Elizabeth (www.capeelizabeth.com/tFort.html)
Great Pond, Cape Elizabeth (www.capeelizabeth.com/tGrea.html)
Portland Symphony Orchestra, Portland (207-773-8191,
     www.portlandsymphony.com)
Two Lights State Park, Cape Elizabeth (207-799-5871)

*Accommodations:*
Inn By The Sea, Cape Elizabeth (207-799-3134)
Inn on Carleton, Portland (800-639-1779, www.innoncarleton.com)
Sheraton South Portland Hotel, South Portland (207-775-6161)
Wild Iris Inn, Portland (800-600-1557, www.wildirisinn.com)

## Castine
*Other Sites of Interest:*
The Wilson Museum, Castine (207-326-9247, www.wilsonmuseum.org)

*Accommodations:*
Castine Cottages, Castine (207-326-8003)
Castine Harbor Lodge, Castine (207-326-4335, www.castinemaine.com)
The Castine Inn, Castine (207-326-4365, www.castineinn.com)
The Manor Inn, Castine (207-326-4861, www.manor-inn.com)
The Pentagoet Inn, Castine (800-845-1701, www.pentagoet.com)

## Cutler/Jonesport/Lubec/Machias/East Machias/South Addison
*Other Sites of Interest:*
Burnham Tavern Museum, Machias (207-255-4432)

**Cutler/Jonesport/Lubec/Machias/East Machias/South Addison** *cont.*
Machiasport Historical Society, Machiasport (207-255-8557)
Quoddy Head State Park, Lubec (207-733-0911, park season;
    207-941-4014, off-season)

*Accommodations:*
Bluebird Motel, Machias (207-255-3332)
Captain Cates B&B, Machiasport (207-255-8812, www.captaincates.com)
Harbor House on Sawyer Cove, Jonesport (207-497-5417, www.harborhs.com)
Little River Lodge, Cutler (207-259-4437, www.cutlerlodge.com)
Margaretta Motel, Machias (207-255-6500)
Quoddy Head Station, Lubec (207-733-4452)

**Deer Isle/Little Deer Isle/Stonington/Swans Island**
*Other Sites of Interest:*
Swan's Island Library & Museum, Swans Island (207-526-4330)
Swan's Island Lobster & Marine Museum, Swans Island (207-526-4282)

*Accommodations:*
Boyce's Motel, Stonington (800-224-2421, www.boycesmotel.com)
Burgess Bed & Bath, Stonington (207-367-2737, www.burgessbedbath.com)
Eggemoggin Inn, Little Deer Isle (207-348-2540)
Eggemoggin Landing, Little Deer Isle (207-348-6115, www.acadia.net/eggland)
The Harbor Watch Motel, Swans Island (800-532-7928, www.swansisland.com)
The Inn at Ferry Landing, Deer Isle (207-348-7760, www.ferrylanding.com)
Inn on the Harbor, Stonington (207-367-2420, www.innontheharbor.com)
Penny's Bed & Breakfast, Stonington (207-367-5933)
Pilgrim's Inn, Deer Isle (888-778-7505, www.pilgrimsinn.com)
Pres du Port B&B, Stonington (207-367-5007)
The Red House Bed & Bath, Little Deer Isle (207-348-5234)

**Friendship/Owls Head/Rockland/Spruce Head/St. George/Tenants Harbor**
*Other Sites of Interest:*
Farnsworth Art Museum, Rockland (207-596-6457, www.farnsworthmuseum.org)
Friendship Museum, Friendship
    (www.midcoast.com/~case/friendshipmuseum.html)
Owls Head Transportation Museum, Owls Head (207-594-4418, www.ohtm.org)
Shore Village Museum, Rockland (207-594-0311)

*Accommodations:*
236 Cedar Bed & Breakfast, Rockland (207-594-5356)
Accommodations at Old Comfortable, Friendship (207-832-4337,
    www.midcoast.com/~case)
The Acorn, Rockland (207-594-0132)
Berry Manor Inn, Rockland (207-596-7696, www.berrymanorinn.com)
Captain Lindsey House Inn, Rockland (800-523-2145, www.lindseyhouse.com)
Craignair Inn, Spruce Head (207-594-7644, www.craignair.com)
East Wind Inn, Tenants Harbor (800-241-VIEW, www.eastwindinn.com)
Harbor Hill B&B, Friendship (207-832-6646)

Lakeshore Inn, Rockland (866-540-8800, www.lakeshorebb.com)
Lathrop House, Rockland (207-594-5771)
Life is Good Bed & Breakfast, Tenants Harbor (207-372-6125,
      www.lifeisgoodbedandbreakfast.com)
Limerock Inn, Rockland (800-546-3762, www.limerockinn.com)
Mill Pond House Bed & Breakfast, Tenants Harbor (207-372-6209,
      www.millpondhouse.com)
Old Granite Inn, Rockland (800-386-9036, www.oldgraniteinn.com)
The Outsiders' Inn B&B, Friendship (207-832-5197)
Trinity on the Ocean Bed and Breakfast, Rockland (207-596-0071,
      www.trinityontheocean.com)
Waterman House and Gardens, Rockland (207-596-0093,
      www.watermanhouse.com)

## Gouldsboro/Milbridge/Prospect Harbor/Winter Harbor
*Other Sites of Interest:*
Bartlett Maine Estate Winery, Gouldsboro (207-546-2408)
Milbridge Historical Museum, Milbridge (207-546-4471,
      www.milbridgehistoricalsociety.org)
Petit Manan National Wildlife Refuge, Milbridge (207-546-2124,
      http://petitmanan.fws.gov)

*Accommodations:*
Acadia's Oceanside Meadows Inn, Prospect Harbor (207-963-5557,
      www.oceaninn.com)
Albee's Shorehouse Cottages, Prospect Harbor (800-963-2336,
      www.theshorehouse.com)
Bluff House Inn, South Gouldsboro (207-963-7805, www.bluffinn.com)
Elsa's Inn on the Harbor, Prospect Harbor (207-963-7571, www.elsasinn.com)
Harbor Treasure Vacation Rental, Winter Harbor (207-963-7086)
Jones Pond Cottages, West Gouldsboro (207-963-7533)
Main Stay Cottages, Winter Harbor (207-963-2601)
Mermaid's Purse Farm Bed & Breakfast and Gallery, Prospect Harbor
      (207-963-7344, www.mermaidspursefarm.com/bb.php)
The Pines, Gateway to Schoodic Point, Winter Harbor (207-963-2296,
      www.ayuh.net)
Sunset House Bed & Breakfast, West Gouldsboro (800-233-7156,
      www.sunsethousebnb.com)

## Isle au Haut
*Other Sites of Interest:*
Acadia National Park, Bar Harbor (207-288-3338, www.nps.gov/acad)
Isle au Haut Village, Isle au Haut (www.keepershouse.com/attractions.htm)

*Accommodations:*
The Inn at Isle au Haut, Isle au Haut (207-335-5141, www.innatisleauhaut.com)
The Keeper's House, Isle au Haut (207-460-0257, www.keepershouse.com)

## Kennebunkport

*Other Sites of Interest:*

Goose Rocks Beach (www.kennebunkport.com/beachgrb.html)
Historic Fishing Vessel the Phyllis A, Kennebunkport (207-967-8809,
    www.phyllisa.org)
Kennebunkport Historical Society, Kennebunkport (207-967-2751,
    www.kporthistory.org)
Seashore Trolley Museum, Kennebunkport (207-967-2712,
    www.trolleymuseum.org)

*Accommodations:*

1802 House B&B Inn, Kennebunkport (800-932-5632, www.1802inn.com)
The Beach House, Kennebunkport (207-967-3850, www.beachhseinn.com)
Bufflehead Cove Inn, Kennebunkport (207-967-3879, www.buffleheadcove.com)
Captain Fairfield Inn, Kennebunkport (800-322-1928, www.captainfairfield.com)
Captain Jefferds Inn, Kennebunkport (800-839-6844, www.captainjefferdsinn.com)
Captain Lord Mansion, Kennebunkport (800-522-3141, www.captainlord.com)
Captain's Hideaway, Kennebunkport (207-967-5711, www.captainshideaway.com)
English Meadows Inn, Kennebunkport (800-272-0698,
    www.englishmeadowsinn.com)
Fontenay Terrace Motel, Kennebunkport (207-967-3556, www.fontenaymotel.com)
Harbor Inn, Kennebunkport (207-967-2074, www.harbor-inn.com)
Inn at Goose Rocks, Kennebunkport (800-457-7688, www.innatgooserocks.com)
Inn on South Street, Kennebunkport (800-963-5151, www.innonsouthst.com)
Kennebunkport Inn, Kennebunkport (207-967-2621, www.kennebunkportinn.com)
The Lodge at Turbat's Creek, Kennebunkport (877-594-5634)
Maine Stay Inn & Cottages, Kennebunkport (800-950-2117,
    www.mainestayinn.com)
Nonantum Resort, Kennebunkport (800-552-5651, www.nonantumresort.com)
The Ocean View, Kennebunkport (207-967-2750, www.theoceanview.com)
Schooners Inn, Kennebunkport (207-967-5333)
Seaside Inn & Cottages, Kennebunkport (207-967-4461,
    http://kennebunkbeachmaine.com)
Shorelands Guest Resort, Kennebunkport (800-99-BEACH)
Tides Inn By-the-Sea, Kennebunkport (207-967-3757, www.tidesinnbythesea.com)
Village Cove Inn, Kennebunkport (888-605-2542, www.villagecoveinn.com)
Waldo Emerson Inn, Kennebunkport (877-521-8776, www.waldoemersoninn.com)
Welby Inn, Kennebunkport (800-773-4085, www.welbyinn.com)
White Barn Inn, Kennebunkport (207-967-2321, www.whitebarninn.com)

## Kittery/York

*Other Sites of Interest:*

Kittery Historical & Naval Museum, Kittery (207-439-3080)
Kittery Outlets, Kittery (888-548-8379, www.thekitteryoutlets.com)
Old York Historical Society, York (207-363-4974, www.oldyork.org)

*Accommodations:*

Anchorage Inn, York Beach (207-363-5112, www.anchorageinn.com)
Coachman Inn, Kittery (207-439-4434, www.coachmaninn.net)

Cutty Sark Motel, York Beach (800-543-5131, www.cuttysarkmotel.com)
Dockside Guest Quarters, York (888-860-7429, www.docksidegq.com)
Enchanted Nights Bed & Breakfast, Kittery (207-439-1489,
    www.enchantednights.org)
Faircrest Motel, York (800-350-4144, www.faircrestmotel.com)
Inn At Long Sands, York Beach (800-927-5132, www.innatlongsands.com)
Inn On the Blues, York Beach (207-351-3221, www.innontheblues.com)
Lighthouse Inn & Carriage House, York Beach (800-243-6072,
    www.thelighthouseinn.com)
Litson Villas, Kittery (800-966-8455, http://litsonvillas.com)
Melfair Farm Bed & Breakfast, Kittery (207-439-0320, www.melfairfarm.com)
Micmac Motel, York (207-363-4944, www.micmacmotel.com)
Portsmouth Harbor Inn & Spa, Kittery (207-439-4040,
    www.innatportsmouth.com)
Stage Neck Inn, York Harbor (800-340-1130, www.stageneck.com)
Union Bluff Hotel, York Beach (207-363-1333, www.unionbluff.com)
York Harbor Inn, York Harbor (800-343-3869, www.yorkharborinn.com)

## Stockton Springs
*Other Sites of Interest:*
Fort Knox, Stockton Springs (207-469-7719)
Fort Point State Park, Stockton Springs (207-941-4014)
Penobscot Marine Museum, Searsport (207-548-2529)
Staples Homestead, Stockton Springs (207-567-3393)

*Accommodations:*
Rocky Ridge Motel, Stockton Springs (207-567-3456)
Memories Made in Maine, Stockton Springs (207-567-4072)

# Bibliography

Jones, Elaine. "A Tribute to the Late Willard Muise." *Boothbay* (Maine) *Register*, 9 November 2000, vol. 124, no. 45.

*Maine Atlas & Gazetteer*. Yarmouth, ME: DeLorme, 2003.

Snow, Edward Rowe. *Famous Lighthouses of America*. New York: Dodd, Mead & Company, 1955.

————. *Famous New England Lighthouses*. Boston: Yankee Publishing Co., 1945.

————. *The Lighthouses of New England*. New York: Dodd, Mead & Co., 1973.

Sterling, Robert Thayer. *Lighthouses of the Maine Coast and the Men Who Keep Them*. Brattleboro, VT: Stephen Daye Press, 1935.

**General Lighthouse Websites:**

American Lighthouse Foundation, www.lighthousefoundation.org.
Cyberlights Lighthouse Page, www.cyberlights.com/lh.
Larry's Lights, www.larryslights.com.
Lighthouse Friends, www.lighthousefriends.com.
Lighthouse Getaway, www.lighthousegetaway.com.
National Park Service Maritime Heritage Program Inventory of Historic Light Stations, www.cr.nps.gov/maritime/park.
New England Lighthouses: A Virtual Guide, www.lighthouse.cc.
United States Coast Guard Maine Light Stations, www.uscg.mil/hq/g-cp/history/WEBLIGHTHOUSES/LHME.html.
www.unc.edu/~rowlett/lighthouse/me.htm.

**Specific Lighthouses:**

Doubling Point Light: www.doublingpoint.org/history.html.
Goat Island Light: www.cyberlights.com/lh/maine/goatisland.htm.
Hendricks Head Light: www.benrussell.com/HH-home.htm.
Kennebec River Range Lights: Range Light Keepers, www.rlk.org.
Marshall Point Light: www.marshallpoint.org/history.html.
Monhegan Island Light: www.briegull.com/Monhegan/lighthousebrochure.pdf.
Portland Head Light: www.portlandheadlight.com.
Seguin Island Light: www.seguinisland.org.
Spring Point Light: www.springpointlight.org.
West Quoddy Head Light: www.westquoddy.com.
Wood Island Light: www.woodislandlighthouse.org.

**Other Sources:**

Acadia National Park, www.nps.gov/acad/.
College of the Atlantic, www.coa.edu.
www.state.me.us/doc/parks/programs/history/fortpownall/pownall.htm.

# Index

# About the Photographer

Paul Rezendes is the photographer of Tide-mark's "Lighthouse Companion Series," including *The Lighthouse Companion for Long Island Sound; The Lighthouse Companion for Massachusetts, Rhode Island, and New Hampshire;* and *The Lighthouse Companion for Maine.* He is also the photographer of *Martha's Vineyard Seasons,* also published by Tide-mark.

Rezendes's other books include the highly acclaimed guide *Tracking & the Art of Seeing: How to Read Animal Tracks and Sign; Wetlands: The Web of Life,* coauthored with his wife, Paulette M. Roy; and *The Wild Within: Adventures in Nature and Animal Teachings.* His photographs have appeared in hundreds of calendars, magazines, books, and catalogs; on posters and cards; and in brochures and promotional materials for corporate and commercial accounts in the United States and abroad. He has worked on assignment for several regional and national magazines, and operates his own stock photography business. A native New Englander, Paul grew up in Westport, Massachusetts, and lives with his wife in a remote forest on the banks of the Millers River in Athol, Massachusetts.

For more information, please contact:

Paul Rezendes Photography
3833 Bearsden Road
Royalston, MA 01368-9400
USA

Tel: (978) 249-8810
e-mail: photos@paulrezendes.com
Website: www.paulrezendes.com